Healing Meditations for Life

David A. Seamands

VICTOR BOOKS

A DIVISION OF SCRIPTURE PRESS PUBLICATIONS INC.
USA CANADA ENGLAND

Acknowledgments

The saintly man who many years ago commissioned us as missionaries to India was Bishop Arthur J. Moore. He had a unique way of saying something when he wanted to give it special emphasis. Instead of raising his voice, or adding an extra gesture or two, he would quietly prefix the statement with, "And now, beloved, I want to say with unbecoming earnestness. . . ."

Following his example I will resist the temptation to use *italics* or CAPITAL LETTERS. Instead, "Beloved, I want to say with unbecoming earnestness," how deeply I appreciate the excellent work Pamela Campbell has done in selecting the excerpts which make up the meditations in this book. She has shown deep sensitivity to the healing themes I consider most important. In the necessary work of occasionally having to rewrite or abbreviate the original text, she has clearly conveyed the meanings I intended. Her Scripture references are very appropriate and the questions for reflection right on target. If you are helped by this book, she deserves a good share of the credit. And so, Pam, "I want to say with unbecoming earnestness," thank you very much for a job well done!

And in the same spirit of gratitude I also want to thank Greg Clouse, Editorial Director of my publisher, Victor Books, for the honor of even considering me as a possible source for such a book. It's one more link in a strong chain with them as coworkers for Christ.

Introduction

I had always been aware that meditation was central to the lives of outstanding Christians throughout history, but thought of it merely as a mystical and subjective devotional experience. It was not until I became more deeply involved in counseling that I discovered how vital it was for the ministry of healing.

In the Scriptures, meditation involves the whole person: thinking, feeling, willing, remembering by visualizing, dialoguing with ourselves and with God. It is an intense, full-person, focused way of incorporating and ingesting truth in order to change both inner attitudes and outer actions. It involves our heads and our hearts, the rational and the emotional, the cerebral and the visceral. Some of our slang phrases describe it best; as when we say, "I need time to *chew* on that," or "It gives me a *gut-level* feeling."

Many years ago the Spirit led me into using the phrase "concept-feelings," or "feeling-concepts," to describe those damaged emotions, distorted perceptions, and dysfunctional relations which cause so much of our brokenness and bondage. I soon discovered that while God often begins our healing with an incredible miracle in some *crisis moment,* true recovery and wholeness is almost always a *gradual process.* God's healing schedule requires genuine meditation on certain therapeutic biblical themes. When we truly "meditate," "reflect," or "contemplate" (NIV margin), every part of our personality is affected, and in turn effects every other part, and we are "being transformed into His likeness with ever-increasing glory" (2 Corinthians 3:18).

I have always defined a Christian counselor as "a temporary assistant to the Holy Spirit." It is from that viewpoint that these "healing meditations" are offered. Rooted in God's Holy Word, I pray they will help the Holy Spirit heal and restore you through the One Isaiah calls "The Wonderful Counselor!"

David A. Seamands

"When the sun was setting, the people brought to Jesus all who had various kinds of sickness, and laying His hands on each one, He healed them."
(Luke 4:40)

At even, ere the sun was set,
The sick, O Lord, around Thee lay;
O in what divers pains they met,
O with what joy they went away!

Once more 'tis eventide, and we,
Oppressed with various ills draw near;
What if Thy form we cannot see?
We know and feel that Thou art here.

O Savior Christ, our woes dispel;
For some are sick, and some are sad,
And some have never loved Thee well,
And some have lost the love they had.

And none, O Lord, have perfect rest,
For none are wholly free from sin;
And they who fain would serve Thee best
Are conscious most of wrong within.

O Savior Christ, Thou too art man;
Thou hast been troubled, tempted, tried;
Thy kind but searching glance can scan
The very wounds that shame would hide.

Thy touch has still its ancient power;
No word from Thee can fruitless fall;
Hear, in this solemn evening hour,
And in Thy mercy heal us all.

Henry Twells, 1823-1900, *The Methodist Hymnal*

Healing

Meditations

for Life

The Last Surrender

"And without faith it is impossible to please God, because anyone who comes to Him must believe that He exists and that He rewards those who earnestly seek Him."   *(Hebrews 11:6)*

After many years of pastoral ministry in which it has been my privilege to counsel people of varying races and cultures, I have come to a strong conclusion that the last thing we humans surrender to God is an admission of our helplessness to save ourselves. We will give up our sins, ambitions, money, name, fame, comfort—we are willing to sacrifice and surrender them all to God. But the most difficult, costly, and last thing we will give up is *our confidence that there is something we can do which will earn us a right relationship with God.*

The second stanza of the hymn, "Rock of Ages," captures our inability so beautifully.

> Could my tears forever flow,
> Could my zeal no languor know,
> These for sin could not atone;
> Thou must save, and Thou alone.
> In my hands no price I bring;
> Simply to Thy cross I cling.

Until the truth conveyed in these lines becomes a living reality, we will not understand or experience the biblical meaning of grace. The writer of Hebrews reminds us that "without faith it is impossible to please God" (11:6). This means that God is not pleased when we attempt to substitute righteousness by achievement through performance for salvation by grace through faith. He will not allow us to change the terms He has set for an acceptable, pleasing relationship with Himself.

"It is by grace you have been saved, through faith—and this not from yourselves, it is the gift of God—not by works, so that no one can boast" (Ephesians 2:8-9). "Not from yourselves. . . so that no one can boast" means that God will not share His glory nor allow us to claim any of the credit for our salvation. Grace is a free gift. The moment we try to pay for it, it ceases to be grace for us.

REFLECTION

In what ways have you tried to achieve through performance a pleasing relationship with God? Have you admitted that you are helpless to save yourself? Why or why not?

God Is in
It with Us

---

*"We have no superhuman High Priest to whom our
weaknesses are unintelligible—He Himself has shared
fully in all our experience."*   *(Hebrews 4:15, PH)*

Of all the words for the Incarnation, the greatest
title is *Emmanuel,* "God with us." God is in it
with us. Better still, God, having gone through
passion and suffering Himself, knows how to be in it and
feel it with us. God doesn't say, "You can come guiltily,"
or "You can come shamefacedly." You never need to feel,
*There's something wrong with me because I'm feeling
depressed; I must not be spiritual.* These are cruelties
we Christians often inflict on one another, and they are
not biblical.

We are not coming into the presence of a neurotic
parent who has to hear only good things from his children. We're not coming into the presence of a father who
says, "Shhh, don't feel that way; that's wrong. Don't cry.
If you keep crying I'll really give you something to cry
about."

We are coming to a Heavenly Father who understands our feelings and invites us to share them with
Him. He understands the frustration, the anxiety, the
depression, the hurts, the feelings of abandonment, loneliness, isolation, and rejection. And what's the proof of
this? The writer of Hebrews says that while Jesus was
human, He "offered up prayers and petitions" (5:7). In a
beautiful, soft quiet time? No! He prayed "with loud cries

and tears to the One who could save Him from death." Jesus knows what it is to pray to God with loud sobs. He wrestled with feelings that nearly tore Him to pieces. He's been through it, and can feel with us. He hurts along with us.

So we can draw near to God with confidence, knowing that we will obtain mercy and find grace in our time of need. We can come when we need forgiveness and when we feel guilty for our sins. And we can also come when we are being racked and tormented by the feelings of our infirmities.

God knows our place of pain and understands it.

R E F L E C T I O N

Is there anything you want to express right now to Emmanuel—"God who is with us in it"? Is there guilt or loneliness or sadness? Fear, frustration, or helplessness? Share those feelings with God in the form of a written prayer.

Beyond Wishful Thinking

"Once you were not a people, but now you are the people of God."   *(1 Peter 2:10a)*

I have spent much of my life listening to the words "if only" in one form or another. Long before I became a pastoral counselor, I heard them during my missionary years (1946-62) in the villages of India. Our work was largely among people on the lowest rung of the Hindu social and economic ladder. In those days, these despised and oppressed people were truly victims of a cruel system made all the more ruthless because their karma or state in life was a divinely prescribed victimization. "If only," they would mournfully intone, "we had been born of high caste parents. If only we owned just a small piece of land. If only we didn't have to live in the segregated section of town. If only we could read and write." You can imagine how revolutionary the Good News was to them with its message of hope.

Although I offered them improvement in education, health, and vocational and agricultural skills, there was something far more important. If these victims were to become victorious over their seemingly hopeless situation, a fundamental inner transformation of spirit had to take place to turn them from futility to faith. One day while I was baptizing a large group of new Christians, the familiar passage of Scripture which I had memorized as a teenager literally exploded with bright new meaning:

But you are a chosen people, a royal priesthood, a holy nation, a people belonging to God, that you may declare the praises of Him who called you out of darkness into His wonderful light. *Once you were not a people, but now you are the people of God;* once you had not received mercy, but now you have received mercy (1 Peter 2:9-10, emphasis mine).

I learned that God could change nobodies into somebodies if only they would give up their "if onlys"! There comes a time in the schedule of God's healing and recovery process when we all have to move beyond hurt to forgiveness, beyond wishful thinking to responsible action, beyond blame to belief. We move into the place where *victims can become victorious!*

R E F L E C T I O N
What are some of your "if onlys" that prevent you from assuming personal responsibility for your actions? Have you moved beyond wishful thinking to responsible action? Why or why not?

So What?

*"And if by grace, then it is no longer by works; if it
were, grace would no longer be grace."*
                                        (Romans 11:6)

I will always remember a turning point in the spiritual life of one of the young teenagers of our church.
He had already made his personal commitment to
Christ. He tried hard but, like most adolescents, was
plagued by the ups and downs in his Christian life. So he
often came forward to the prayer altar during the invitation time following church services. He had done so once
again after a Sunday night service conducted by a visiting
evangelist. Soberly he shared with me his determination
"to make it this time." Then he asked, "But what if I fail?
What happens if I fall?"

I replied, "Steve, I've come to know you pretty well.
Probably better than anyone in the church. So I think I
can guarantee you one thing—*you will fail, you will fall.
So what?*"

He looked up at me a bit shocked. He had expected
me to reassure him, not give him a guarantee of failure. I
could see he was thinking over the implications of my
"So what?"

And then very slowly he began to smile and to nod
his head.

"Hmmm...I think I see what you mean. I think I'm
catching on," he said. "Of course I'm going to fail; sure
I'll fall. *But that really doesn't make any difference, does*

it?" And then the smile lit up his whole face.

Of course, a lot of growth followed, but that was his initial discovery of the way of grace. And his discovery—that with grace, failure doesn't make any difference—changed his life. It was a joy to watch him grow in grace. Later, he became a dispenser of grace as a pastor for eleven years, and now teaches about grace as a professor of systematic theology in a seminary. Are you wondering about my strange reply that I was sure he would fail because I knew him so well? That's because I happen to be his dad!

R E F L E C T I O N
How often do you worry about failing or falling? How do you respond to the ups and downs of your spiritual life? Are you a dispenser of grace? Why or why not?

The Inner
Rings of Life

"Surely He took up our infirmities and carried our sorrows...and by His wounds we are healed."
(Isaiah 53:4-5)

I f you visit the western United States, you will see those beautiful giant sequoia and redwood trees. Naturalists can show you a cross section of a great tree they have cut, and point out that the rings of the tree reveal its developmental history, year by year. Here's a ring that represents a year when there was a terrible drought. Here's where the tree was struck by lightning. Here are some normal years of growth. This ring shows a forest fire that almost destroyed the tree. Here's another of savage blight and disease.

And that's the way it is with us. Just a few minutes beneath the protective bark, the concealing, protective mask, are the recorded rings of our lives.

There are scars of ancient, painful hurts...as when a little boy rushed downstairs one Christmas dawn and discovered in his Christmas stocking a dirty old rock, put there to punish him for some trivial boyhood naughtiness. This scar has eaten away at him, causing all kinds of interpersonal difficulties.

Here is the discoloration of a tragic stain that muddied all of life...as years ago behind the barn or out in the woods, a big brother introduced his little sister to the mysteries—no, the miseries of sex.

And here we see the pressure of a painful, repressed

memory. . .of running after an alcoholic father who was about to kill the mother, and then of rushing for the butcher knife. Such scars have been buried in pain for so long that they are causing hurt and rage that are inexplicable.

For many of us, uncovering the memories of our past is very painful. But the truth is, healing begins at the point of pain. Somewhere between our sins and our sickness lies an area Scripture calls "infirmities." These problems require a special kind of prayer and a deeper level of healing by the Holy Spirit. As we begin to understand that these infirmities are not subject to ordinary prayer, discipline, and willpower, we will begin to live more compassionately with ourselves and others.

R E F L E C T I O N
In what ways have you been avoiding the pain of your past? What are some past experiences on the rings of your life that cause you to feel a sense of hurt or sadness? As you reflect on those painful experiences, what part of God's character brings the greatest sense of comfort and security to you?

Dammed-Up Feelings

"When I kept silent, my bones wasted away through my groaning all day long." *(Psalm 32:3)*

When I was eleven years old, my missionary parents brought my brother and me home on furlough. The next year Mother and Dad went back to India. We thought we would see them in a few years, but along came World War II and they got stuck in India. The next time I saw my parents was on my twentieth birthday!

At that time I didn't realize that layers of unexpressed feelings were being buried. Not until I married did I discover what I was really like: a lonely, frightened little boy, who could not express his deepest feelings. Oh, yes, I could in sermons, and I could listen sensitively when I counseled others. But I couldn't express my feelings to the one I wanted to more than any other, my wife.

In the early days of our marriage, when we went to India as missionaries, I would go out in my Jeep to the villages and be gone for weeks at a time. I remember saying to myself, *This time when I get home it's going to be different. I'll take Helen in my arms and say, "Honey, I love you."* But the minute I got to the door, I froze. That old childhood wall came between us.

I needed to share my deepest self with Helen, that frightened, lonely little boy with all of his weaknesses. I'd been scared to do that all of my life. Helen could express her feelings; she told me her fears and how people got her down. But not I. I was always brave. When Helen expressed inadequacy, I interpreted it as feminine weakness. I was afraid that if I ever told her how I really felt, we would both dissolve!

But one day the dam broke and I shared my real self, the terrified, lonely kid inside of me. I told Helen everything, at times sobbing uncontrollably. And you know, I found out that she was amazingly strong. She sustained me and gave me strength. And best of all, when my false front cracked and she saw what I was really like, then I could express my love freely. The logjam was broken and I could express my deepest feelings, both positive and negative.

R E F L E C T I O N
How would you describe your real self? With whom can you share your real self?

The Deception
of Low Self-Esteem

"I praise You because I am fearfully and wonder-fully made."　　　　　　　*(Psalm 139:14a)*

An uneasy sense of self-condemnation hangs over many Christians like a Los Angeles smog. They find themselves defeated by the most powerful psychological weapon that Satan uses against Christians. Its name? Low self-esteem. Though they understand their position as sons and daughters of God, some Christians are bound by a terrible feeling of inferiority and chained to a deep sense of worthlessness.

Learning to recognize Satan's deception can help us break out of a vicious circle of fear and uselessness. Here are four ways that Satan uses this weapon to bring defeat and failure into our lives.

First, low self-esteem paralyzes our potential. I have witnessed the watered-down living, the wasted gifts, the leakage of a veritable gold mine of human power and possibility. And inwardly I have wept. Do you know that God also weeps over it? He is not so much angry as He is grieved.

Second, low self-esteem destroys our dreams. We can't live *in* our dreams, we can't live *on* our dreams, but we do live *by* our dreams. With the wrong kind of vision about ourselves, we will surely self-destruct, and God's great plan for our lives will not be fulfilled.

Third, low self-esteem ruins our relationships. If we consider ourselves inferior or worthless, we will think that God really must not love and care for us. Such thinking often leads to those inner questions and resentments which begin to foul up our relationship with God. Low self-esteem also spoils our relationships with other people. When we devalue ourselves, we become overly absorbed *in* and *with* ourselves, and we don't have anything left over to give to others.

Finally, low self-esteem sabotages our ability to serve the body of Christ. What is the first thing people say when asked to perform some Christian service?

"Teach Sunday School? I can't stand up in front of people."

"Sing in the choir? Why don't you ask Mary? She has a much better voice."

The problem with low self-esteem is that it robs God of marvelous opportunities to show off His power and ability through our weaknesses. Remember, we are seen by God as being so precious that we are infinite in worth.

R E F L E C T I O N

What situations trigger your sense of being of less value than other people? How would you describe your self-esteem? In what way might low self-esteem be sabotaging your relationships?

In Deep Anger

"He looked around at them in anger and deeply distressed at their stubborn hearts."
(Mark 3:5a)

Christ's anger was never more accurately expressed than when He was about to heal the man with the withered hand on the Sabbath. In Mark 3:5, we find the only place in the New Testament which actually uses the word *anger* to describe Jesus.

I believe that Christ's anger was part of His very perfection. For to say that Christ never got angry would demonstrate a great flaw in His divine character. The Bible speaks often of the anger of God—365 times, in fact.

It's high time some of us get over our childish ideas on this subject. Anger is not a sinful emotion. In fact, there are no sinful emotions—only sinful *uses* of emotions. And there are many of us who misuse our emotion of anger. Anger is a divinely implanted emotion. Closely allied to our instinct for right, it is designed to be used for constructive spiritual purposes.

The person who cannot feel anger at evil is a person who lacks enthusiasm for good. If you cannot hate the wrong, it's very questionable whether you really love righteousness.

Anger is not weakness; rather it is great strength. The Bible nowhere condemns anger as a feeling. It does condemn the wrong quality of anger and warns us against inviting, nurturing, or holding on to that kind. And it plainly condemns many wrong actions which are likely to follow such angry feelings.

However, anger which fulfills the same conditions that Jesus' anger did is the right kind. Such anger must be directed at something that is obviously wrong and evil. It must be controlled, well in hand, and under the direction of the will—not simply a heated passion out of control. And perhaps most important of all, there must not be in it any malice, bitterness, resentment, or hate.

REFLECTION

What kinds of childish ideas have you had about anger? Are you guilty of any misuses of anger? On a scale of 1 to 10, would you say your anger is closer to outbursts of childish rage (1) or to controlled emotion under the direction of the will (10)?

Descent into Hell

"For we do not have a High Priest who is unable to sympathize with our weaknesses."
(Hebrews 4:15a)

I n a lifetime of listening to hurting people, I have heard many personal descents into hell with its abyss of emotional pain. Again and again, I have found that the most therapeutic turning point in the healing process is when people discover that God not only knows and cares but also *understands how they feel.*

As I write, the face of one counselee comes to mind. It had been a second marriage for Ashley and her husband, involving children from both sides. Later they had a child of their own. Things went well for many years until his alcoholism and infidelity shattered her dreams. He finally left and moved in with the other woman. It was in the midst of the divorce and a complicated custody settlement that he became more hateful and seemed to go out of his way to hurt her at every point. The most painful blow came in court when he accused her of not loving one of *his* children, now a teenager. I'll never forget her anguished look and broken tone of voice when she told me how she had taken over that youngster when he was just a toddler.

"Dr. Seamands, I loved that kid with all my heart. I quit my job to stay home and care for him. He had been so neglected he was downright emaciated, and my heart went out to him. I literally poured my life and my love into him as if he were my very own. And now to be accused in court of not loving him—oh, I can't tell you how much that hurt me. It felt like a knife in my stomach."

Her tears flowed freely with every word. The miracle was that in spite of her deep hurt and anger, she never allowed bitterness or resentment to establish a beach-head in her heart. How was this possible? Because every time we prayed together, we would remind ourselves that our Lord too had been betrayed, abandoned, falsely accused, and had cried out in agony. We knew that He knew how she felt and that every feeling could be unashamedly shared with Him.

Reflection

What are some ways that your dreams have been shattered? What difference would it make to know that God knows, cares, and understands your deep disappointment?

I ' m   S o   L o n e l y !

"God sets the lonely in families."

(Psalm 68:6a)

I 've heard it innumerable times in my counseling
ministry from some of the finest Christian singles I
have known:

"Doc, I was so lonely. I was OK during the week when
I was working, but I just dreaded to see Friday afternoon
come because the weekends were so terrible. The most
awful kind of loneliness would come over me—it was
almost physical, like a blanket or something. It would
surround me—I could almost feel it. I got so I just had to
be with someone, anyone, and before I realized it I was
doing things I never thought I'd do, just to have somebody. I'm ashamed to tell you, it was literally some
body—just a body to *touch me and hold me.*"

We've trained our youth and young adults to cope
with all kinds of difficulties—all but one, loneliness. We
especially need to prepare future Christian workers to
handle this. I have listened to the agonizing confessions
of many unmarried missionaries whose lives were moral
and clean as long as they were in the protective fellowship of Christians. But in some distant place, waves of
loneliness lapping away at their moral shorelines eroded
their souls, until the undertow of emptiness and sexual
desires pulled them under and almost drowned their
faith.

Sometimes the most painful kind of loneliness is that

of the married person who is physically in the same house with a husband or a wife, but emotionally miles apart. Communication has broken down, or the wife has become too engrossed in caring for a child, or the husband is too busy in his work—even God's work—and one partner fails to meet the emotional needs of the other. Soon someone is lonely, although surrounded by people—children, neighbors, church members. The marriage partner is filling one side of the bed but not the emptiness of the spouse lying so close. That's when the evil one fills even the finest of imaginations with forbidden fantasies and sows the seeds of powerful temptations. Never underestimate the intricate connection between loneliness and sexual temptation.

R E F L E C T I O N

What kinds of connections have you experienced between loneliness and sexual temptation? How do you cope with loneliness?

Treasured Dreams

"For where your treasure is, there your heart will be also."   *(Matthew 6:21)*

In his book, *The Heart of a Champion,* Olympic medalist Bob Richards tells about the famous runner, Charley Paddock. One day while speaking in an assembly at a Cleveland high school, Charley said, "Who knows, we may even have an Olympic champ right here in this hall!"

Afterward, a skinny, spindly-legged black youngster who had been hanging around the edge of the crowd came up and said to him very shyly, "I'd give anything if I could become a championship runner someday."

Charley answered him warmly, "You can, Son, you can, if you'll make it your goal and give it your all."

In 1936 that young man, whose name was Jessie Owens, won gold medals and broke records in the Munich Olympics. Adolf Hitler watched his stunning performance and was infuriated, for the fulfillment of that dream did as much as anything to smash his idiotic dream of a superior Aryan race.

When Jessie Owens came home they gave him a ticker-tape welcome. That day another spindly-legged black youngster squeezed his way through the crowds and said, "I'd sure like to grow up and become a runner in the Olympics someday."

And Jessie remembered and grabbed the kid's hand and said, "Dream big, Son, dream big. And give it all you've got." In 1948, Harrison Dillard won gold medals at the Olympics.

A high school student was practicing the high jump in preparation for the state contest. Each time his coach would raise the bar a little higher. Finally, he put it up to the record height for that event. The teenager protested, "Aw come on, Coach, how do you think I can ever jump *that high?*"

The coach replied, "Just throw your heart over the bar first and the rest of you will follow."

In Matthew 6:21, Jesus hinted that there was something that even preceded the heart. If *heart* reflects desires, then *treasure* represents the value we put on the object of those desires. It is the prize, the goal, the treasure for which we are willing to pay any price.

R E F L E C T I O N

What are some of your goals? What are you doing to reach those goals? For what prize, goal, or treasure are you willing to pay any price?

The Grace-
Based Life

"Grace and truth came through Jesus Christ."
(John 1:17b)

A grace-based, grace-oriented life is a pattern of *being,* a manner of perceiving, thinking, feeling, willing, acting, reacting, and relating. Such a way of life is more than a basic experience of Christ, such as conversion and the new birth, or being filled with the Spirit, or experiencing occasional times of spiritual highs. A lifestyle which becomes God's *right* way of *being* is lived out as the right way of *doing*—coping with life's situations and relationships. The opposite of a grace-oriented life—a performance-orientation—is also an all-inclusive way of *being,* resulting in a *wrong* way of coping with life and relating to people. It's important that we see both the problem and the solution in this same light—as all-pervasive *wrong* and *right* ways of living life and relating to people.

I want to make it clear there are no quick cures, no speedy solutions. Neither a miraculous Christian experience nor an instantaneous inner healing is likely to free one from the bonds of a performance-oriented life, especially in its extreme pefectionistic forms. No one believes more than I do in the necessity of the new birth and life in the Spirit as *the* basic ingredients of the Christian life. However, I also believe that many Christians with damaged emotions and unhealed memories need a special kind of inner healing to enable them to live truly victorious lives.

Gaining a better understanding of the nature of your problem will not free you from the unhealthy and frustrating performance treadmill. As important as insight and knowledge are, they do not automatically heal or change. However, awareness and insight are of tremendous help in showing us *what* we need to look for and *how* we need to pray. They also reveal those areas of our lives where we need healing grace in order to fully live out the saving and sanctifying grace we have experienced in Christ. While healing grace may at times include points of crisis, it will always be a process of changing our patterns of life.

R E F L E C T I O N

What are some times when you have been disillusioned by instant spiritual cures? On a scale of 1 to 10, would you describe your lifestyle as more performance-oriented (1) or more grace-oriented (10)? Why?

The Guiding Lights

"Continue in what you have learned and have become convinced of, because you know those from whom you learned it, and how from infancy you have known the holy Scriptures, which are able to make you wise for salvation through faith in Christ Jesus."
(2 Timothy 3:14-15)

God gives us five great lights for guidance in special times of decision when we need more specific direction.

Guidance comes through:

❖ God's Word
❖ outer circumstances (open and closed doors)
❖ our own best reasonable thinking
❖ the counsel of other Christians
❖ the inner voice of our feelings.

No good ship's captain would just go by one light in the channel. He would crash his ship on the rocks or wreck it on a sandbar. Not even two lights or three lights. The trained navigator lines up all of the lights, and then knows he is in the clear, deep channel, and that he can sail safely to his destination.

I remember talking with a missionary pilot just after he had completed a long and difficult course to get his license for instrument flying. After he told me about it, one idea stuck in my mind. He said, "You know, instrument flying is so different from ordinary flying by sight, because you have to learn that you just can't fly by your perception. Sometimes you have to go against your feelings. You just keep your eyes on those instruments. Sometimes you feel as if you are going opposite of what the instruments tell you. You sure can't fly by your feelings."

And you can't fly the Christian flight by your feelings either. Keep your eyes on the instruments: God's Word, your own best thinking, the outworking of circumstances, and your inner feelings. As much as possible, balance them all together. Put off that childish overdependency on feelings and impressions as the basis for guidance.

R E F L E C T I O N

In what ways have you been over- (or under-) dependent on your feelings for guidance? To what sources of guidance do you go when you need help making important decisions?

GOD IS NEVER MORE

INVOLVED IN OUR

LIVES THAN AT TIMES

OF DISAPPOINTMENT

AND DESPAIR.

Every Personality Has a Face

"As he thinketh in his heart, so is he."
(Proverbs 23:7a, KJV)

Many years ago, a famous plastic surgeon, Dr. Maxwell Maltz, wrote a best-selling book, *New Faces—New Futures*. It was a collection of case histories of people for whom facial plastic surgery had opened the door to a new life. The author's theme was that amazing personality changes can take place when a person's face is changed.

However, as the years went by, Dr. Maltz began to learn something else, not from his successes but from his failures. He began to see patient after patient who, even after facial plastic surgery, did not change. People who were made not simply acceptable, but actually beautiful, kept on thinking and acting the part of the ugly duckling. They acquired new faces but went on wearing the same old personalities.

In 1960, Dr. Maltz wrote another best-seller, *Psycho-Cybernetics*. He was still trying to change people, not by correcting jutting jawbones, or smoothing out scars, but by helping them change the pictures they had of themselves.

Dr. Maltz says it's as if every personality has a face. This emotional face of personality seems to be the real key to change. If it remains scarred and distorted, ugly and inferior, then the person continues to act out a role, regardless of the change in his physical appearance. But if the face of his personality can be reconstructed, if the old emotional scars can be removed, the person can be changed.

I am absolutely amazed at the way self-image influences our actions and attitudes, and especially our relationships with other people. What is self-image or self-concept? Your self-image is based on a whole system of pictures and feelings you have put together about yourself. I like to use the compound words *feeling-concepts* or *concept-feelings*. For self-concept includes both mental pictures and emotional feelings. This is at the very core of your personality. The way you *look at* yourself and *feel about* yourself, way down deep in the heart of your personality—so you will be and so you will become. What you see and feel will determine your relationship with people and with God.

R E F L E C T I O N

What feelings do you have about yourself? How is the way you look at and feel about yourself affecting your relationships with other people? Your relationship with God?

Six Principles for Healing

"Come near to God, and He will come near to you."
(James 4:8a)

What is our part in the healing of our damaged emotions? Let me suggest six general, biblical principles.

1. *Face your problems squarely.* With rigorous moral honesty, and with God's grace, you can confront that awful, hidden childhood memory, however deep the feelings within you. Acknowledge it to yourself and to another human being.

2. *Accept your responsibility in the matter.* "But," you say, "I was a victim." True enough. But what about your response? What about the fact that you learned to hate or resent, or to escape into an unreal world? Life is like a complicated tapestry. Heredity, environment, all the things experienced in childhood from parents, teachers, playmates—all these things together with your responses weave the design of your life. You will never receive healing until you accept *your* responsibility.

3. *Ask yourself if you want to be healed.* Do you really want to be healed, or do you just want to talk about your problem? Do you want to use your problem to get sympathy from others? Do you just want it for a crutch, so that you can walk with a limp?

4. *Forgive everyone who is involved in your problem.* The reason some people have never been able to forgive is that if they forgave, the last rug would be pulled

out from under them and they would have no one to blame. Jesus made it very plain that no healing occurs until there is deep forgiveness.

5. *Forgive yourself.* Many Christians say, "Yes, I know that God has forgiven me, but I can never forgive myself." How can you really believe that God has forgiven you, and then not forgive yourself? When God forgives, He buries our sins in the sea of His forgiveness and His forgetfulness. We have no right to dredge up anything that God has forgiven and forgotten.

6. *Ask the Holy Spirit to show you what your real problem is, and how you need to pray.* The Holy Spirit prays in and through us, and makes intercession for us. Sometimes the Holy Spirit uses a temporary assistant in the form of a human counselor. Other times the Spirit is able to help us perceive what the real problem is through God's Word or through some sudden incident in our lives.

R E F L E C T I O N

With which of these six principles might you struggle most? Why?

A Depressed Christian?

"Because of the Lord's great love we are not consumed, for His compassions never fail."

(Lamentations 3:22)

Depression is a common experience among Christians. You may ask, "How can that be? A depressed Christian? The very words are contradictory. If a person has been truly born of and filled with the Spirit, then shouldn't it be impossible for him to be depressed? Surely, the fact that a Christian would be suffering from depression is a sign that something needs to be straightened out with the Lord. It must be a sign of sin in that person's life."

Now all of that may sound very good and simple, but it does not stand the test of Scripture, the facts of Christian experience, or the truths about psychology.

Have you read one of David's psalms recently?

"My soul is downcast within me" (Psalm 42:6).

Have you listened to Elijah?

"I have had enough, Lord....Take my life" (1 Kings 19:4).

Have you heard Jonah?

"Take away my life, for it is better for me to die than to live" (Jonah 4:3).

Have you thought about Jesus' words in Gethsemane?

"My soul is overwhelmed with sorrow to the point of death" (Matthew 26:38).

Can you find better descriptions of depression—a depression in which the person almost despaired of life itself?

The Scriptures are much more realistic and kind to us than some Christians are, as they clearly show that it is possible for Christians to be very depressed. Depression is related to personality structure, physical makeup, body chemistry, glandular functions, emotional patterns, and learned feeling-concepts. People who are extremely introspective and sensitive often have the worst problems with depression. As Christians we must realize and accept this. Our failure to deal realistically with ourselves regarding depression is the root cause of much of our depression.

The first step in learning to live above depression is to accept yourself as you are. I urge you to accept your personality and acknowledge your temperament. Having truth in the inward parts means you no longer resist who you are. You stop fighting your temperament as an enemy and begin to accept it as a gift from God. While you cannot change your temperament, you *can* allow it to be controlled by the Holy Spirit.

R E F L E C T I O N

Are you a person whose personality is subject to depression? How have you learned to deal with depression?

All or Nothing

"My prayer is not for them alone. I pray also for those who will believe in Me through their message."
(John 17:20)

I have counseled well over a thousand people who have been troubled with the problem of perfection- ism and find that most of them have an "all-or-noth- ing-at-all" outlook. Their world only has two colors— pure white or jet black. If they don't achieve perfection, then they are total failures. This keeps them on emotion- al and spiritual highs and lows.

I've often wondered whether or not Simon Peter didn't have a touch of this. Did you ever notice his "all- or-nothing-at-allness"? On the Mount of Transfiguration he was afraid, but he wanted to build booths and stay up there forever. At the Last Supper he said to Jesus, "Lord, You're not going to wash my feet." But when Jesus rebuked him, "OK, Lord, wash not only my feet, but my head and my hands." He swung from "Not even my feet!" to "Give me a bath!"

In those last hours Jesus said that someone was going to betray Him. Peter declared, "Lord, though everybody else in the whole world would deny You, I'll die for You!" Within a few hours when a maid kidded him a little, he scoffed, "Who? Jesus? Why, I've never even heard of the man. Who's He?"

Aren't you glad that Jesus Himself said to someone like Peter, "Simon, Simon, behold Satan has desired to have you that he may sift you as wheat. But I have prayed for you that your faith may not fail, and when you have turned again, strengthen your brethren" (Luke 22:31-32, RSV). And in the same patient way, Jesus Himself has prayed for you too (John 17:20) and is even now interceding for you (Hebrews 7:25). Through His Spirit He is here to help you, even as He helped Peter through his many mood swings and spiritual ups and downs. And, just as He finally was able to get Peter leveled off so that the unpredictable and unstable Simon became Cephas, a rocklike apostle, so He will do the same for you.

R E F L E C T I O N

What kinds of mood swings and spiritual ups and downs have you experienced? Do you have a sense of Jesus' prayers and intercession for you in times of emotional defeat?

What's Your Motive?

"The Lord searches every heart and understands every motive behind the thoughts."

(1 Chronicles 28:9b)

When young Christians share their dreams with me, they often say something to the effect that they "want to do great things for God." They don't want to be "ordinary," to be "just one more"— whatever it is. I appreciate the spirit behind this but sense the danger. They envision themselves largely in the realm of achievements and accomplishments—*doing,* whereas God wants to refine those dreams so that they are balanced with the *being* which comes through relationships—both with God and with other people. Jesus said to His disciples, "I no longer call you servants [but] friends" (John 15:15). We need to have both the intent and the content of our dreams deepened by the maturity that only time and testing can bring.

Let me share something with those of you who are young in years or in the faith—something which has been one of my most painful experiences of growing older. As I look back on many of the accomplishments I once considered among the best in my service for God, I am often shocked as the Spirit reveals to me how mixed my motives were. There was far more of "self" in them than I was aware of at the time. Far more desire to accomplish speedy results than to achieve satisfactory relationships. Again and again God refined those motives by allowing me to go through some painful experiences. Isn't this what He is trying to tell us through His Word?

> When all kinds of trials and temptations crowd into your lives, my brothers, don't resent them as intruders, but welcome them as friends! Realize they come to test your faith and to produce in you the quality of endurance. But let this process go on until that endurance is fully developed, and you will find you have become men of mature character with the right sort of independence (James 1:2-4, PH).

R E F L E C T I O N

How would God evaluate the motives behind some of your dreams? Through what kinds of painful experiences has God refined your motives?

Parental Grace

"The Word became flesh and made His dwelling among us. We have seen His glory, the glory of the One and Only, who came from the Father, full of grace and truth."   *(John 1:14)*

A mother was trying to reassure her little girl as she put her to bed in a darkened room.
"Honey, you don't need to be scared. Remember God is going to be right here with you."

The little girl replied, "I know, Mama, but I need a God with skin on Him."

Children don't think in abstract concepts but in concrete pictures. A young child's world is very physical, very literal. Ideas and mental concepts come later. For them, words need to become flesh and blood, skin and bodies, faces and eyes which smile, feet that walk, hands that touch, arms that hug. The strongest influences on them come through real live human relationships with people they consider important.

Parents are the most effective communicators of truths, values, concepts, and lifestyles, because they incarnate them in concrete relationships. This is the reason I have said children learn a language of relationships long before they learn to speak a single word.

This is why parental grace is so incredibly important. Through it, we get our earliest experience of genuine— though imperfect—*agape* love. Through it, we can grow up experiencing a quality of grace similar to what we receive from God Himself. This taste of love and grace, though partial, whets our appetite and prepares us for God's perfect love and the advent of His saving grace in our lives. However, it does not guarantee our salvation, for we can still refuse to respond to God or receive His gift.

I believe that God intended parental grace to be the chief means of counteracting the Fall. In fact, it operates by the same principles God used in the Incarnation. However, even the best possible Christian parenting cannot make a child's nature morally neutral or spiritually good, nor can it guarantee that the child will automatically choose the right.

Christian parents who overload themselves with guilt need to remember something—Adam and Eve were the only people who ever had *perfect parenting* and yet they chose the wrong!

R E F L E C T I O N

If you are a parent, how have you struggled with expressing grace to your children? What quality of parental grace did you experience while growing up?

What You've
Always Wanted

---

*"For He chose us in Him before the creation of the
world to be holy and blameless in His sight. In love
He predestined us to be adopted as His sons through
Jesus Christ."*   *(Ephesians 1:4-5a)*

L inda was a battered child, abused physically and
sexually by her own brothers and a stepfather.
This had filled her with deep shame and low self-
esteem which had plunged her deeper into sin. Finally
she ran away from home and ended up at eighteen years
of age in New York City. She was alone and had very few
friends.

One night, literally in a den of evil and practically
naked, she was sitting on a chair in a room. In the same
room, a couple was engaged in sexual intercourse. A dev-
astating sense of loneliness and guilt swept over her. The
terrible realization of *where she was* and *who she was*
and the fact no one really cared overwhelmed her. She
suddenly realized the utter selfishness of the scene—
everyone there was using each other and using her. It hit
her like a thunderbolt and filled her with awful black-
ness, depression, and despair.

But in the midst of that situation there came (what
she called) an overshadowing sense of the presence of
God. The thought arose within her like an inner voice, "I
love you, I always have, and I always will. I really care for
you and love you."

She turned around, knelt at the chair, and putting her

head in her hands began to sob. "O God, fill my emptiness. Please love me the way I've always wanted to be loved."

That was a beginning. Within a month she underwent a dramatic conversion.

"I experienced a flooding," she told me, "a sense of God's complete forgiveness. And most of all, what I'd really wanted all my life—a clean heart."

Reborn and restored, she got help, returned home, and was reconciled to her mother. Eventually she became the instrument through whom God reached several family members.

Today, Linda is a pastor's wife and a radiant, Spirit-filled Christian. God is always first on the scene. Long before even "the creation of the world," His grace had Linda in mind.

R E F L E C T I O N
What are some times when you have had a strong sense of God's presence? What is it that you've wanted all your life?

The Hidden
Child in Us All

*"When I was a child, I talked like a child, I thought like
a child, I reasoned like a child. When I became a man, I
put childish ways behind me."*

(1 Corinthians 13:11)

Somewhere, sometime, you were a child. Although
you don't remember all the details of your childhood, the child and teenager you once were is still
important to you today because it continues to exist
within you.

During my first year as pastor of the Wilmore
Church, I took turns with other county pastors giving live
devotions on a nearby radio station. The fifteen-minute
program started daily at 9:15. Every ten or twelve weeks
it fell my turn. One day I was delayed and rushed over to
the radio station, arriving at 9:12 all out of breath. Three
minutes later I gave the devotions.

After the program was over I walked out and the
young secretary looked up at me and said, "Rev.
Seamands, we like to have the speaker here at least ten
minutes ahead of time, if you please." My face flushed
and I blurted out with a lot more emotion than I ever
intended, "Well, I made it on time, didn't I?"

She looked a bit startled, but didn't answer because I
was on my way out the door.

*Who in the world does that saucy little blonde think
she is, anyhow? Doesn't she realize the busy schedule of
a minister, how much time the program takes, how it*

ruins the morning?

Then all of a sudden something dawned on me.

Seamands, what in the world has upset you like this?

Now, when your response to a situation is way out of proportion to the event (like mine was), you'd better suspect the little child within you is acting up.

With a surprising amount of feeling and emotion, I realized that I hadn't been talking to that impertinent little blonde in the radio station but reliving an incident from my childhood. All the feelings of a hurt little boy came out in that conversation.

When I saw it so clearly, I was able to ask the Holy Spirit to move in and take the sting out of the memories so that it would be no longer operative in my life. The next day I apologized to the young lady, to clear both my conscience and the atmosphere at the radio station.

R E F L E C T I O N

What are some situations where your response was way out of proportion to the events? Are you able to associate any childhood experiences or feelings with those events?

From Almost
to Altogether

"So you are no longer a slave, but a son; and since you are a son, God has made you also an heir."
(Galatians 4:7)

John Wesley, an ordained Anglican clergyman and the founder of Methodism, was a devout seeker after personal holiness. But despite all his sacrificial service and good works, he did not find peace with God, and called himself "an almost Christian." Then on May 24, 1738 he discovered grace, while listening to someone read Martin Luther's *Preface to the Book of Romans.* In Wesley's now well-known words:

> About a quarter before nine, while he was describing the change which God works in the heart through faith in Christ, I felt my heart strangely warmed. I felt I did trust in Christ, Christ alone, for salvation; and an assurance was given me, that He had taken away my sins, even mine, and saved me from the law of sin and death.

Wesley said that he became "an altogether Christian," and that whereas before he had the religion of a "servant," now he had that of a "son."

How many of us have been thinking and feeling and living not like a family member should, but like a servant does?

❖ The servant is accepted and appreciated on the basis

of what he does, the child on the basis of who he is.

❖ The servant starts the day anxious and worried, wondering if his work will really please his master. The child rests in the secure love of his family.

❖ The servant is accepted because of his workman-ship, the son or daughter because of a relationship.

❖ The servant is accepted because of his productivity and performance. The child belongs because of his position as a person.

❖ When a servant fails, his whole position is at stake; he might lose his job. When a child fails, he is grieved because he has hurt his parents, but he is not afraid of being thrown out. His basic confidence is in being loved, and his performance does not change the stability of his position.

Every time you find yourself feeling and living as a servant, you can stop and remind yourself, saying: "Father, I am your child, and I'm going to live and feel like one!"

R E F L E C T I O N

Have you been living more like a servant and less like a child of God? Why or why not?

The Forgiven Self

"He Himself bore our sins in His body on the tree, so that we might die to sins and live for righteousness; by His wounds you have been healed."
(1 Peter 2:24)

I have written much about the healing of the memories. Not long ago I was suddenly struck with the thought that God too has had a healing of His memories. In one sense, the Cross involves the mystery of God's memory. There are several places in the Scriptures which imply that God no longer remembers our sins against us: "Remember not the sins of my youth and my rebellious ways" (Psalm 25:7) and "Do not hold against us the sins of the fathers" (Psalm 79:8).

In commenting on this remarkable fact, Corrie ten Boom puts it in her own inimitable way, "When God forgives He forgets. He buries our sins in the sea and puts a sign on the bank saying, 'No Fishing Allowed.' " The most helpful word I ever heard on this was from a young man who said every time he started to pray, he would remind God of a certain failure in his past. One day when he started to do this it was as though God whispered to him, "My son, enough of that. Stop reminding Me of that sin. I distinctly remember forgetting it a long time ago!"

The first step toward Christian adulthood is to be done with any subtle form of inner penance and self-condemnation for already forgiven and forgotten sins. The guilty self needs to become the forgiven self.

REFLECTION

Are you continuing to remind God of certain failures in your past? If so, which ones? If you placed your guilt on the crucified Christ, do you think you would experience a true sense of forgiveness? Why or why not?

Enduring Temptation

"No temptation has seized you except what is common to man. And God is faithful; He will not let you be tempted beyond what you can bear."

(1 Corinthians 10:13a)

James tells us to consider it a joy when we fall into various temptations. He even goes so far as to say that the man who endures temptation is blessed. However, that is not our usual view of the matter, and with some people it is made much worse by a fundamental confusion of temptation and sin. Let us look carefully at the Scriptures and some practical aspects of temptation so that we will not fall prey to Satan's slimy suggestions which keep us feeling guilty and under condemnation.

First, let us forever fix in our minds that everybody experiences temptation. Dante had an allegorical picture of the Christian life as a journey in which a man climbed up a winding mountain road. When he began the journey, he was a young man. After he had climbed a short while, a snarling wolf leaped out of the bushes and tried to tear him to pieces. To Dante this was the wolf of lust, of bodily passion, and represented the major temptation of youth.

As he climbed higher and came into middle life, a giant tiger sprang on him. This was the tiger of pride, and represented the great temptation of middle age—pride of position, of name, and of great status. Finally, near the top, at the time of old age, a great, hairy-maned lion came bounding after him. This was the great temptation of later life—money and financial security.

In his classification of the three great temptations of life the point Dante was trying to make is this: There is no level of Christian life where you will be free from temptation. There is no person, however Spirit-filled, however saintly and mature, who will not face temptation of some kind.

R E F L E C T I O N

Have you ever thought that there might be a higher level of spiritual experience where you might not have to face temptations anymore? With which of the three classifications of temptation do you struggle the most?

The Division of Labor

"If anyone has caused grief. . .you ought to forgive and comfort him, so that he will not be overwhelmed by excessive sorrow." (2 Corinthians 2:5, 7)

Denny was obviously very upset when he sat down before me. "I just don't understand," he said with almost a tinge of anger in his voice. "I went to a retreat two weeks ago and the Spirit forced me to face up to the fact that I had not truly forgiven Mike. Though it was a struggle, God gave me the grace to really forgive him. And I've had wonderful peace in my heart since then. But within the last few days, a lot of those old feelings have come back and I've been overwhelmed by them. That's surprised me. I guess I didn't really forgive him. I thought I had. Maybe I'll have to do it all over again; but to be honest with you, I'm afraid it's not going to work this time either."

This is a common experience for many Christians and one of those areas where we need to know the truth and be set free from unnecessary confusion, guilt, and condemnation. We must first make sure that we understand the division of labor involved in forgiving others. There is a human part, something only we can do. And there is a divine part, something only God can do.

This division of labor means we cannot do God's part and God cannot do our part. We get into trouble if we try to do what only God can do. And we get into equal trouble if we ask God to do what He has ordained that only we can do. The human part is the crisis of our will. The divine part is the process of changing our feelings.

The crisis of our will simply means that there comes a time and a place where we have to make a definite decision as to whether or not we are willing to forgive the wrongdoer. God's part—changing our feelings—is a process that usually takes time to accomplish. Sometimes God seems to peel off layers of feelings as old memories return and new ones arise. All of a sudden we remember some other wrongs and former wounds are reopened. But as we once again, in an act of fresh obedience to God, reiterate our original decision to forgive and release these fresh hurts to God, He keeps replacing the old feelings with new ones in an ongoing process.

REFLECTION

Is there someone who has wounded you deeply that you would like to forgive? In what ways have you struggled with old memories and feelings about this person?

A Secret Life

"I have chosen the way of truth; I have set my heart on Your laws." *(Psalm 119:30)*

The ringing of the telephone awakened me out of a deep sleep. The caller was Beth, wife of a former student. She was all apologies when she realized I was in a different time zone, but when I heard her story, I was glad she had called.

Beth's husband, Stan, was a born leader, a gifted preacher, and had already built up a large congregation who loved him very much. So I was shocked when she told me with tears in her voice that Stan was going to quit the ministry.

"He's already made up his mind. He's written a letter of resignation and plans to give it to the elders this week and announce it from the pulpit next Sunday."

Unknown to her, Stan had had a longstanding problem with pornography; recently, quite by accident, a church member had seen him buying some porno magazines in a distant city. Stan was ashamed and afraid, and his conscience troubled him greatly. He opened his heart to Beth and told her of his lifelong battle with sexual fantasies. Also, he shared that of late he had begun to mentally yield to them and allow for the possibility of some "inappropriate behavior" with women in the church. He was grateful that God had restrained him, but he was feeling unworthy to be a minister. He thought the only solution was to resign as their pastor.

As I talked to Stan over the next few days, I told him I thought the devil was trying to push him into punishing himself and destroying his ministry. I advised him to call his elders and confess everything to them privately. Then, if they wanted him to stay, he should request them to hold him accountable in the future.

Reluctantly and fearfully he did this, and the elders were completely sympathetic. They very much wanted him to continue and agreed to meet with him regularly. He is still at that church and God has given him an even greater ministry—beginning with some of the elders who, touched by his honesty, began to deal with their own deep needs. Beth certainly struggled with personal disillusionment and some shattered dreams. But through forgiveness, open communication, and further counsel, her dreams for both their marriage and their ministry have been rebuilt.

R E F L E C T I O N

Do you have any painful secrets that you feel you need to hide from the significant people in your life? What prevents you from opening your heart to your spouse or family?

THERE ARE NO

SINFUL EMOTIONS—

ONLY SINFUL *USES*

OF EMOTIONS.

Love Is an Action, Not a Reaction

"We love because He first loved us."
(1 John 4:19)

Grace is God's love in action toward those who do not deserve it. And this love is manifested as grace, offered us in the life and death of Christ. Hence God does not say:

> I love you *because*...
> I love you *since*...
> I love you *forasmuch as*...
>   or,
> I will love you *if*...
> I will love you *when*...
> I will love you *after*...
> I will love you *provided*...
> I will love you *presuming*...

Any such statement would make His love conditional, would mean His love was caused by something in us—our attractiveness, our goodness, our lovableness. The reverse of this would mean there could be something in us which would stop God from loving us. God's love for us is unconditional; it is not a love drawn from God by something good in us. It flows out of God because of His nature. God's love is an action toward us, not a reaction to us. His love depends not on what we are but on what He is. He loves because He is love.

We can refuse the love of God, but we cannot stop Him from loving us. We can reject it and thus stop its inflow into us, but we can do nothing to stop its outflow from Him. Grace is the unconditional love of God in Christ freely given to the sinful, the undeserving, and the imperfect.

REFLECTION

Have you ever felt that there is something within you that might prevent God from loving you? How do you feel about the statement that "we cannot stop Him from loving us"? In what ways have you tried to refuse the love of God?

Our Healer Understands

"He was despised and rejected by men, a man of sorrows, and familiar with suffering."

(Isaiah 53:3a)

To understand what it cost Jesus to be our Healer, listen to His prayers in Gethsemane. Can you hear them, as if for the first time? He "began to be sorrowful and troubled. Then He said to them, 'My soul is overwhelmed with sorrow to the point of death'" (Matthew 26:37-38).

Wait a minute, Jesus. Do You mean to say that You experienced such feelings, such emotions and pain in that wretched hour, that You even wanted to die? Do You mean to say that You understand when I am so depressed that I no longer want to live?

If you have battled terrible loneliness, or pathological emptiness, if you have experienced the blackest bouts of depression, you know that when you are in the pits, the hardest thing to do is to pray, because you do not feel God's presence. I want to assure you that He knows, He understands, and He shares all your feelings because He has been through them.

Now follow Jesus into His trial. "Then they spit in His face and struck Him with their fists. Others slapped Him" (Matthew 26:67).

When I counsel people, I often ask, "Tell me, what's the worst picture in all of your memory, the one that comes most often to bring you pain?" Their eyes start to fill with tears; soon the overflow comes down the cheeks, and before long, even strong, strapping men are shaking with pain and anger.

"It was when Dad would lash out and hit me on the head."

"It was when Mother would slap me."

Nothing is more destructive to a human personality than a slap in the face. It is so humiliating, so demeaning, so deeply dehumanizing. It destroys something very basic to our personhood.

But our wounded Healer understands. He knows what it is to be struck on the head, to be slapped in the face. He is touched with the feelings that arise in you from that hurt. He wants you to know that He is not angry with you about your feelings. He understands.

R E F L E C T I O N

In what ways do you identify with the pain Jesus experienced during His arrest? What hurtful memories bring you emotional pain? Deep inside, do you believe that there is not a single feeling you cannot bring to God?

D r e a m s   A r e
C o n t a g i o u s

"Where there is no vision, the people perish."
(Proverbs 29:18a, KJV)

I personally experienced the infectious power of a dream some years ago. In 1963, I was in my first year of the pastorate and had been working very hard to get the public schools of our county racially integrated. I was getting rather discouraged due to the large opposition. One cold winter day I marched with several thousands who had come from all over the state to take part in a rally on the steps of the Kentucky state capitol.

I had heard a lot about the speaker of the day and was hoping he might further our cause. He began by summarizing the national civil-rights movement and some of its goals. Then slowly, like a symphony increasing in intensity, his words and emotions gained momentum. I sensed a change as the crowd began to stir and express their own feelings. I had seen something like this in India during the struggle for independence, and I knew what could happen to a large mass of people. So I decided I would remain strictly an observer. Whatever the others did, *I was not going to blow my cool. I simply would not be moved.*

But then Dr. Martin Luther King, Jr. reached his crescendo. "I HAVE A DREAM!" he shouted exultantly, and tearing his own heart wide open so we could all peer inside, he showed us a picture of that dream. Again and again he repeated the resounding refrain, "I HAVE A

DREAM!...I HAVE A DREAM!"

Each time he would include a fiery Old Testament quotation and add one more picture of the dream. Finally, like a movie camera zooming in closer and closer until its object fills the whole wide screen, he showed us the full picture of his dreamscape. It was so electrifying that I found myself clapping and shouting, "Amen... yes...that's right...Amen!" It was an unforgettable experience. That day I learned the awesome power of an awe-inspiring dream, and I returned home lifted and encouraged.

Without a dream or a vision people really do perish; but *with* one they withstand persecution, persist through opposition, and pursue the prize with perseverance.

R E F L E C T I O N

Recall a time when you experienced the awesome power of another person's dream. Did you feel excited, terrified, or somewhere in between? What dream or vision has God planted in your heart?

Feelings Just Are

"In your anger do not sin."   *(Ephesians 4:26a)*

There's no such thing as a bad feeling or a good feeling. Feelings just *are.* They are consequences of a whole range of things that come out of your personality. No emotions are in themselves sinful. What you do with them will determine whether they are wrong or right. How you handle them will determine whether they lead you to righteousness or to sinfulness. The emotions themselves are a very important part of your God-given personality equipment.

One emotion that many people generally consider bad is *anger.* I grew up on some unbiblical, inhuman, and destructive preaching about anger always being an unsanctified emotion. It took me years to get over those attitudes. They almost destroyed my Christian life and nearly wrecked my marriage, because I had to learn how to properly express my anger to my wife.

In Mark 3:5 we read that Jesus became angry. While this is the only place in the New Testament that actually *says* Jesus got angry, I think we can safely assume that Jesus was angry when He whipped the money changers out of the temple (Mark 11:15-18). Never was Jesus more divine than at those moments when He was expressing white-hot anger. Many times, perfect love and anger go hand in hand; indeed, the anger is the result of perfect love.

We Christians have a semantic trick that often confuses people. "Oh, that's not anger; it's 'righteous indignation.'" Why don't we just come out and say that there is a right use of anger, and that anger in itself is not a sinful emotion.

What matters is your use of anger—how you express it and how you resolve it. But when you have this unreal, false expectation that you must never experience or never express any feelings of anger, you become a perfect setup for emotional wreckage and depression.

Anger is a divinely implanted emotion, part of God's image in the human personality, and is to be used for constructive purposes.

R E F L E C T I O N

Is it difficult for you to express certain emotions? Which ones? Why? Think of a time when you used anger in a constructive way. How did you express it and how did you resolve it?

Group Grace

"For where two or three come together in My name,
there am I with them." (Matthew 18:20)

J ack and Lucille and their two children had traveled
quite a distance to attend the conference. I counseled with Lucille just once and, with her permis-
sion, had prayed that God would reveal her true need.
The conference closed with a general time of witnessing
to what God had done for us. After several had shared,
Lucille arose and through tears said to the group:

> I don't understand what's wrong with me. All week
> I've run from all of you. Each message made me more
> miserable, and each group more uncomfortable. Yet
> all of you have been wonderful to me. You've tried to
> love me, but I just wouldn't let you. I've watched love
> overflow for me out of my husband all these years,
> but it's only made me all the angrier. My little girl has
> tried to love me, but I've slapped her around. This
> week I've finally admitted to myself that what I've
> really wanted all my life was to be loved and to love.
> But I've never been able to do it, because I've never
> been able to accept God's love. I've resented God and
> I haven't even been grateful for a wonderful husband
> and two wonderful kids. And this week I've seen all of
> you love my little girl, and the way she's responded to
> your love, and it's been so amazing. And it's made me
> so empty.

By now she was almost screaming.

Oh God, please forgive me. I've been so proud, so hard, and so unloving.

A well-meaning minister interrupted her, saying, "Let's all sing a song together." But Lucille immediately spoke.

No, no, let me go on. I'm just starting, and I want to finish. O thank You God. I'm free! I'm free! It's gone. I feel free for the first time in my life. Thank You, God!

Meanwhile, Lucille's little girl who was in the nearby childcare room had heard her mother crying out. She came running into the room and said, "O Mama, Mama, what's wrong?" and with a leap jumped up and started hugging her mother around the neck. By now her husband, Jack, was also weeping, and the three began hugging each other. It was an electrifying moment.

Lucille had been a Christian and in the church for many years, but was finally untied and set free only by the power of group grace.

R E F L E C T I O N

Consider a time when you have experienced group grace. What attitudes and behaviors were evidenced by the group?

An Unsafe Bridge

"The rain came down, the streams rose, and the winds blew and beat against that house; yet it did not fall, because it had its foundation on the rock."
(Matthew 7:25)

Finished early in 1940, the Tacoma Narrows Bridge in Washington State was a masterpiece of engineering. A 2,800-foot suspension bridge, it provided a much-needed crossing over the waters of the Puget Sound. It cost $75 million, a staggering expenditure at the time. It attracted so much attention that a local insurance company used it as an advertising slogan. Ads reading, "As Safe as the Tacoma Bridge," helped its insurance business flourish—but only for a few months.

On November 7, 1940, a high wind began blowing in the Sound, and no one knows exactly what happened next. One theory was that because of the unusual terrain, wind trapped in that location would actually have the effect of doubling in velocity. So the 42-mile-an-hour wind of that afternoon had the effect of 84 miles an hour.

Whatever the cause, the bridge began to sway slightly. That was nothing new—the media had already affectionately named the bridge "Gallopin' Gertie." But this time the swaying got steadily worse until the bridge was in a violent front-and-back oscillation. Terrified drivers climbed out of their vehicles and crawled back on the highway bridge which was now like a washboard. Within minutes the gigantic structure splintered into pieces and crashed into the Sound. Fortunately, the only loss of life was one animal.

The embarrassed insurance company had to hire anyone they could find, at ridiculously high wages, to go all over the Northwest to take down their ad. When the bridge was finally rebuilt in 1951, the engineers gave special attention to remedy what they felt might have been the original defect, "insufficient torsional and vertical stiffness in the main girders which were only eight feet deep."

Many a sincere Christian has tried to bridge the gap between God and himself by way of obedience to a precise and codified set of rules. The precisely engineered scheme of externalized laws, rules, and regulations gives the appearance of immense strength. But the person's efforts never bring lasting peace because there is always one more rule that some person or group adds to the list. This is an unsafe bridge which will one day collapse in a storm.

R E F L E C T I O N
In what legalistic ways have you tried to bridge the gap between God and yourself? What were the results?

Bad News/
Good News

*"But now He has reconciled you by Christ's physical
body through death to present you holy in His sight,
without blemish and free from accusation."*
                                    (Colossians 1:22)

A farmer who had experienced several bad years
went to see the manager of his bank.
    "I've got some good news and some bad news to
tell you. Which would you like to hear first?" he asked.

"Why don't you give me the bad news first and get it
over with?" the banker replied.

"OK. With the bad drought and inflation and all, I
won't be able to pay anything on my mortgage this year;
either on the principle or the interest."

"Well, that is pretty bad."

"It gets worse. I also won't be able to pay anything on
the loan for all that machinery I bought, nor on the principle or interest."

"Wow, that is bad."

"It's worse than that. You remember I also borrowed
to buy seeds and fertilizer and other supplies. Well, I
can't pay anything on that either—principle or interest."

"That's awful—and that's enough! Tell me what the
good news is."

"The good news," replied the farmer with a smile, "is
that I intend to keep on doing business with you."

There's some rather profound theology in that story,
provided we reverse the subjects. The good news of the

Gospel is that in spite of our total moral bankruptcy, *God keeps on doing business with us.* Notwithstanding the hopelessness of our predicament, God has found a way to restore us to a relationship with Himself and to bring healing to the damaged areas of our personalities.

R E F L E C T I O N

What hope do you find in the statement that "God keeps on doing business with us"? In what parts of your personality would you like to experience healing?

The BIG
Little Verse

"Jesus wept."   *(John 11:35)*

The Gospel of John was written primarily for Greeks who believed that the chief characteristic of God was *apatheia,* the total inability to feel any emotion. Theologians have argued for centuries that God is immutable, perfect and, therefore, He cannot really *feel* our pain.

In their remarkable book, *In His Image,* Dr. Paul Brand and Philip Yancey present this issue in a different and helpful light. They say that such an idea is too Western, too allied to Greek philosophy. The Hebrew viewpoint is quite different. They suggest there may be a way to put both of these truths together by considering the human brain with its remarkable paradox concerning pain. Because the brain has no nerve endings which record pain, the brain itself cannot feel any pain. Yet, the pain center of the entire body is in the brain. All pain from any place in the body passes through the brain, and that's how we *feel* it. Anesthesia doesn't actually stop the nerve ending from *feeling* the pain; it stops the brain from *recording* it, and so we don't *feel* it. Perhaps, they say, God and our pain are something like that. Because Christ is the "Head of the Body," we can in one sense say *He feels no pain.* But in another sense we can say *He feels all pain,* including yours and mine, since all pain passes through Him.

To John's Greek readers, for God to show emotion

would deny His omnipotence and be unworthy of what a deity was suppose to be. But that didn't faze John, for he reveals a totally different picture of God. John 11:35, "Jesus wept," is the shortest verse in the Bible. When I was a boy in Sunday School, it was one of my favorites. In those days I never dreamed how BIG that little verse really is, how important and how tremendous the theological truth wrapped up in two small words. It has taken me a lifetime to realize what a massive door swings upon those two tiny hinges. It is the door which opens into the very heart of God, revealing that behind this universe is a *caring heart of suffering love.*

R E F L E C T I O N

Do you believe that God feels all your pain? Why or why not? What picture of God do you get from the phrase, "Jesus wept"?

Jazz & Ice-Cream Evangelism

"I am the way and the truth and the life. No one comes to the Father except through Me."

(John 14:6)

One night in 1960, a handsome young man knocked at the door of our home in Bangalore, India. He introduced himself as a student at the university working on a Ph.D. in electronics. He was interested in American jazz and said he had heard we had a stereo and a good collection of records—like the classics of Glen Miller and others.

That kind of highly arranged jazz has always been a hobby of mine. I invited him in and within minutes we were listening to the music of the big band era and eating some of Helen's delicious fridge-made ice cream. This began a close friendship with the youth who turned out to be from a wealthy, high-caste Hindu family. He was a long way from his parents and felt lonely and homesick.

His visits continued for more than a year without any mention of religion. Then one night, as we were listening to the "King of Swing," Benny Goodman, he suddenly said, "Could we talk in your office?"

As soon as we were alone, he asked: "Brother David, what does it mean to be a Christian?"

I shared with him very briefly, then loaned him a book by C.S. Lewis and a tape by E. Stanley Jones. We had many times of discussion together. He was concerned not to deny the good things his parents had taught him. Again and again, I had to assure him that to receive Jesus Christ was not a denial of the good ethical teachings he had received, but to find in Him their true fulfillment.

Finally one night he surrendered himself to Christ. A few months later, he received Christian baptism. He paid a heavy price for his decision, because his orthodox Hindu family immediately disinherited him. But to this day he is a dedicated Christian. Helen and I look back with joy on what we called our "jazz and ice-cream evangelism days" when, as interpreters for God, we had to translate what people *wanted* into what they really *needed.*

R E F L E C T I O N

What are some times when you have shared what it means to be a Christian with a nonbeliever? What resources would you recommend to a person seeking answers to the meaning of Christianity?

The Renewing Process

"I am making everything new!"

(Revelation 21:5b)

I heard a beautiful testimony from one of the converts in a Bill Glass Prison Crusade in the South. He was a huge man with his arm in a sling. They told us he was known as one of the tough guys of the prison. He accepted Christ as his Savior on the first night of the crusade. A few days later he said, "You know, something's happening to me. I don't really understand it and I sure can't explain it. I got up this morning and I didn't scream and holler like I usually do. Even my cellmates commented about it. The only way I can describe it is it's like someone took the old tape which had been playing in my mind since I was a kid and put a new tape in and it's playing new talk and new music."

This was an amazing insight for a comparatively uneducated person. He was already beginning to experience the renewing and reprogramming process. Sometime later he discovered another important factor and added, "But you know, I've got to keep working on it and see to it that the right tapes are playing."

He had discovered his responsibility. Just in case anyone has gotten the wrong idea from anything I've said—the reason we try to discover damages from the past is not to blame someone else. Rather, it is to clarify our insights and outline the real issues, so that we can direct our prayers and efforts to the right places.

Jesus had an amazing way of cutting through all excuses and attempts to scapegoat others. He always made people face up to their responsibilities. If we were all honest we would agree that the problem is really in ourselves. Just as the fingers and the thumb are rooted in the palm of the hand, so our problems are rooted in the self. And this self needs the spiritual experiences of forgiveness, healing, and surrender to come into wholeness.

R E F L E C T I O N

How has God's redeeming grace broken through the chains of your sinful past? Are there some areas from your past where you need to focus less on blaming and more on clarifying and outlining the real issues? What are they?

Truthful Speech

"As servants of God we commend ourselves in every way. . .in truthful speech and in the power of God."
(2 Corinthians 6:4a, 7a)

Debbie wanted to serve supper by candlelight two or three times a week. Bob would say, "I like to see what I'm eating!" or "Are you trying to poison me?" This little conflict grew until it became a big one.

Every time Debbie used candles, Bob let her know that he just didn't like it.

"Candlelight again?. . .Well, I just don't like that. . . . But go on, have your candles!"

Of course, that ruined the meal and left Debbie hurting. They never talked about it. It was candlelight versus noncandlelight.

During a communication exercise at one of our marriage enrichment seminars, Debbie opened up.

You see, she had been a foster child, and the people who finally raised her were very poor. They ate in the kitchen on a bare table. The only light in the room was one light bulb without a shade. It just hung there and swung back and forth every time the kitchen door opened. As a teenager, Debbie had vowed to herself, "When I get married I'm going to have a beautiful house with a separate dining room, and we are going to eat by soft light."

When Debbie had finished telling Bob all of this, he

was really broken up.

"O Honey," he said, "you can have all the candles you want! I understand now."

Well, when he understood about the candles, it turned out that she didn't need to have them so often anymore. That is usually the case! All we really want is for someone dear to understand where we are coming from.

R E F L E C T I O N

What kinds of communication problems do you experience in your significant relationships? Does your spouse or closest friend understand where you are coming from? Why or why not?

The Real You

"Surely You desire truth in the inner parts; You teach me wisdom in the inmost place."

(Psalm 51:6)

Somewhere in the process of growing up, a child receives messages about himself, about God, about other people, and about relationships. If those messages are negative, a child unconsciously begins to believe the following: "I am not accepted and loved as I am. I can only be accepted and loved *if* I become someone else."

The tragedy is that the person's God-designed self-hood—the Real Self—doesn't ever get a chance to grow. All the emotional and spiritual energies which ought to go into the development of his God-intended self are used to create the Super Self—a false, idealized picture of himself. The Super You is an imaginary picture of who you think you have to be in order to be loved and accepted. This distortion extends even to God to whom you must somehow present only your good side.

When you come into the presence of God in meditation or prayer, which of the two do you present to Him? What's the picture of yourself that you are bringing to God?

I asked that once of a successful evangelist. The man was silent for an unusually long time. Then he said to me, "You know, I've never really thought of it that way before. But to be honest with you, I'm afraid that I always go into the presence of God with my best spiritual foot forward and my finest halo on. I have to admit that when I imagine myself in the presence of God, I'm always Super Me. I don't think I have ever gone as Real Me, just as I am."

When you waste time and energy trying to be Super You, you rob yourself of growth and the friendship of God. And you never let God accept and love the Real You for whom Christ died. You can be yourself in Jesus and you need not compare yourself to anyone else. He wants to heal *you* and to change *you* in order that the Real You can grow up to be the person He intended you to be.

R E F L E C T I O N

In what ways have you changed your outer self (the way you look, act, think, and feel) in order to gain other people's love and acceptance? Which self do you present to God—your Super Self or your Real Self?

Irregular People

"All things are possible with God."
(Mark 10:27b)

I used to have an antique roll-top desk. I loved it, with all its little compartments, drawers, and pigeonholes for my office supplies. At least it enabled me to keep my mess organized. Remembering it leads to my confession. As I look back at my early years as a new Christian, I see that in my zeal to be all-out for Christ I pigeonholed people, classifying them spiritually so that they fit into neat categories. There were the "Saved," the "Spirit-filled," the "Worldly," the "Shallow," and so on. I made pigeonhole graves which entombed people. The truth was that the pigeonholes entombed *me,* and I cheated myself out of fellowship and enrichment with a lot of wonderful Christians. Even worse than that, I kept some unreached people wrapped in the grave clothes of their sins, instead of allowing the life-giving power of Christ to work in their lives.

Eugenia Price, well-known Christian speaker and author, tells in *The Burden Is Light* of the part her friend Ellen Riley played in her conversion and subsequent growth in grace. With deep appreciation she recounts how Ellen stuck by her, in spite of the fact that she kept up her incessant chain-smoking and slipped into profanity. Even when she had a bad setback and denied everything for a brief period, Ellen stood by her, sometimes at considerable risk to her own spiritual reputation. Listen to what Eugenia says about Ellen in *Discoveries Made from Living My Life:*

> I testify from my own experience that if the one who led me to Christ had in any way, by the merest shadow of inference, chanced to condemn me during those first tense days as the Holy Spirit worked in my heart, I would not be writing these lines now.

> How grateful I am for the way God forced me to expand my horizons by simply dumping me into so many different situations, with so many different kinds of people with whom He was obviously working in so many different ways. Slowly but surely, my narrow and limited view of God and His methods became enlarged. How much my life has been enriched by discovering the incredible ways God uses to get through to people!

R E F L E C T I O N

Do you have trouble maintaining a hopeful, redemptive attitude toward other people? Why or why not? In what ways has your view of God and His methods expanded since you became a Christian?

Inward Emptiness

"For you know that it was not with perishable things such as silver or gold that you were redeemed from the empty way of life handed down to you from your forefathers, but with the precious blood of Christ, a lamb without blemish or defect."

(1 Peter 1:18-19)

A few years ago we had an older student in the seminary—who had given up his rank as a senior officer in the Naval Air Force to enter the ministry. One day I heard him tell how this came about.

He said that from his early youth he had a dream about being in the Navy and was determined to reach the top of the ladder. He had worked hard and his dream had come true. His next promotion would be to Admiral.

But one day God, working through the changed lives of transformed people, had drawn back the veil and shown him the shocking truth. As he so aptly put it, "Although I had indeed reached the top of the ladder, I suddenly realized the ladder was leaning against the wrong building!"

His dreams had turned out to be false and empty mirages. Although his *wants* had been fulfilled, his deepest *needs* could be met only when Christ entered his life.

We need to be on the lookout for those whose outward status and success hide deep inward emptiness. We must ask the Holy Spirit for the wisdom to take people where they are, to express what they think they want, and to interpret those wants so that they will come to discover what they really need.

How are your "wants" different from your "needs"? In what ways have you used status or success to hide inner emptiness? Are you willing to accept people where they are? Why or why not?

GOD CAN DO

ANYTHING EXCEPT

NOT BE GOD!

Gut-Level Grace

"Refresh my heart in Christ."

(Philemon 20b)

A sound theology of grace can literally be purely *propositional* or all in the head, and not *visceral* or in the heart. We think the term *gut-level* is fairly modern and realistic. But it's fascinating to remember that people in Bible times considered the stomach, the belly, as the source of deeply experienced beliefs and emotions. And so those passages which we translate with *heart,* the older *King James Version* translates with *belly* and *bowels.*

- ❖ "Out of his belly shall flow rivers of living water" (John 7:38, KJV).
- ❖ "If there be therefore any consolation in Christ...any comfort...any bowels and mercies" (Philippians 2:1, KJV).
- ❖ "Yea, brother, let me have joy of thee in the Lord; refresh my bowels in the Lord" (Philemon 20, KJV).
- ❖ "But whoso hath this world's good[s] and seeth his brother have need, and shutteth up his bowels of compassion from him, how dwelleth the love of God in Him?" (1 John 3:17, KJV)

In biblical days, the word *bowels* was used exactly as we use *gut-level* now. Much more than mere emotions, it also included attitudes and actions and deeds, and was an all-pervasive way of thinking, feeling, doing, and relating. It meant that the whole personality was affected, right down to the deepest levels.

Today, many Christians have a sound biblical doctrine of grace to which they give full mental assent. It is a truth they believe about God, but it is not their gut-level basis of living with God, themselves, and others.

Our theological and mental grasp of grace needs to penetrate our innermost being and become gut-level grace. Of course, there are barriers to grace which have been implanted in many people. These barriers include ideas which operate in the conscious level of the personality. But they also include feelings, habits, attitudes and reactions, predispositions and presuppositions which have been conditioned by the memories and patterns of prior experiences and relationships.

Most of these sensations operate from the deep subconscious level of the personality. They are mental images so intertwined with emotions that each one affects the other. They need to be penetrated by the Gospel; in many instances, they require healing grace in addition to a renewal of the mind.

R E F L E C T I O N

Do you feel that your mental grasp of grace has penetrated to a "gut-level" grace? Why or why not?

Long-Stemmed
Compliments

"For whoever exalts himself will be humbled, and who-
ever humbles himself will be exalted."
(Matthew 23:12)

Pride, as it is used in the Bible, is a dishonest estimate of ourselves. Paul warns against this, "For
by the grace given to me I say to every one of
you: Do not think of yourself more highly than you
ought, but rather think of yourself with sober judgment,
in accordance with the measure of faith God has given
you" (Romans 12:3).

Just as Paul reminds us we are saved by grace
through faith and that not of ourselves, he here reminds
us that God's grace and our faith will also give us an honest and accurate estimate of ourselves. In both instances,
pride is excluded, because the grace and the faith are
both gifts from God. As Paul so incisively asks, "For who
makes you different from anyone else? What do you have
that you did not receive? And if you did receive it, why
do you boast as though you did not?" (1 Corinthians 4:7)

Someone once asked Corrie ten Boom how she could
possibly handle all the compliments and praise that were
constantly heaped upon her, without becoming proud.
She said she looked at each compliment as a beautiful
long-stemmed flower given to her. She smelled it for a
moment and then put it into a vase with the others. Each
night, just before retiring, she took the beautiful bouquet
and handed it over to Jesus saying, "Thank You, Lord, for

letting me smell the flowers; they all belong to You." She
had discovered the secret of genuine humility.

Humility means that while I like myself and appreciate the affirmation of others, I don't need to prove my
worth to God, myself, or others. Healthy Christian self-
esteem rests on the firm foundation of knowing we are
accepted, loved, and appreciated by God Himself. This
generates in us a humility which is born out of gratitude
for His undeserved grace and which comes from God.
Feelings of inferiority, insecurity, and inadequacy do not
come from God, but from Satan, as a counterfeit for true
humility.

R E F L E C T I O N
Are there times when you feel the need to prove your
worth to God? To yourself? To others? What person(s) in
your life have demonstrated genuine humility?

The Direction of the Will

"*My Father, if it is possible, may this cup be taken from Me. Yet not as I will, but as You will.*"
(Matthew 26:39b)

A young lady who came to me for counseling was deeply in love. But she was beginning to realize that, as much as she loved the young man, he was not the right one for her because of some genuine spiritual differences that she saw as insurmountable. So she wrote him a letter, they talked about it, and then she broke it off.

Some days later she came to me in tears, depressed, all torn up. What was wrong? Well, she had some well-meaning friends who assured her that there must be something wrong with her spiritually or she wouldn't be having such a struggle. She was crying a lot, couldn't do her work, and wasn't concentrating on her studies. She knew she had done the right thing and didn't have the slightest intention of going back on her decision, but her feelings were giving her a rough time. Instead of helping her bear the burden, her well-intentioned but misinformed friends had added a burden of spiritual guilt to her already overburdened heart.

I said to her, "Honey, of course, you can cry. Of course, you are feeling blue. Of course, you are struggling. But tell me, what is the direction of your will?" She replied at once, "That hasn't changed, because I know what I must do."

We read together the story of Christ's struggle in the Garden of Gethsemane. She saw the point. Her commitment to God's will was firm and steady. But her emotions were battered and putting up a struggle.

When I am in conflict, the best thing I can do is take my feelings to God in ruthless honesty and tell Him what they really are. Then I reaffirm the full surrender I made many years ago and apply it to this specific situation.

You can surrender your will. You can make the all-out surrender now if He has readied you for it. But it is not the end. Rather, it is an open end, in which you begin a lifetime process of specific surrenders to the Lord.

R E F L E C T I O N

How do you respond to inner conflict? Have you ever played the role of the well-intentioned but misinformed friend to someone struggling? How could you be a better friend in a similar situation?

Missing the Boat

"Being confident of this, that He who began a good work in you will carry it on to completion until the day of Christ Jesus." *(Philippians 1:6)*

Years ago, before the days of the automobile, there was a minister who, although retired, still loved to preach. One week he received two invitations for the same Sunday morning. He wanted to preach both times and discovered, to his great joy, that he could, because of the timing of the two churches. One was an early service at nine o'clock and the other at eleven. However, he would have to catch the ferry to cross the river which separated the two sections of the town in which the churches were located.

He timed it perfectly. Finishing the first service a little early, he walked down toward the river as fast as he could to catch the 10:30 ferry. Alas, as he rounded the corner the boat was just leaving the dock. The ferry was only a few feet or so out in the water, so he shouted to the people on deck, and taking a flying leap he jumped—and landed safely on the deck of the ferry.

His momentum propelled him into the arms of a big, burly man who caught him and held him there as he puffed and panted breathlessly. Then the man looked at him and asked in a disgusted tone, "What in the world are you doing? This boat's not going out. It's just coming in!"

And so it is with our damaged dreams and hopes. Sometimes, it appears that we have missed the boat, but

God makes all this a part of His plan and His schedule. Oswald Chambers, the great devotional writer, referred to God as the "Engineer of our circumstances." There is more at work than just the forces of evil which we can see so plainly. God is never more involved in our lives than at these times of disappointment and despair.

R E F L E C T I O N

What are some times when your dreams were damaged or delayed, resulting in disappointment? Did you feel that God was at work in your life at those times? Why or why not?

Dealing with Depression

"Now is your time of grief, but I will see you again and you will rejoice, and no one will take away your joy."
(John 16:22)

You might be surprised to learn that Martin Luther wrote a great deal about depression. Because of his unhappy childhood, because of an overbearing, strict, religious upbringing, Martin Luther had a constant battle with low self-esteem and depression. He offered a lot of wonderfully up-to-date suggestions about meeting this problem. Let me share a few of his, and some of my own, which I have found to be most helpful.

Avoid being alone. When you are depressed you don't want to be around people. But withdrawing means isolation, and isolation during depression means alienation. Force yourself to be with people.

Seek help from others. Real friends can help you gain perspective. Seek out people and situations which generate joy.

Sing! Make music. This was the only cure for King Saul's moods of depression. The harmony and beauty of David's music lifted King Saul's spirit of depression (1 Samuel 16:14-23).

Praise and give thanks. All the saints of the centuries agree on this one. When we can't feel God's presence or really pray, we can thank God for the leaf on the tree or the beautiful wing of a bird.

Lean heavily on the power of God's Word. God can use any portion of Scripture to minister to you during times of depression, but throughout the centuries His people have found the psalms to be the most beneficial.

Rest confidently in the presence of God's Spirit. The psalmist repeatedly affirmed the secret of deliverance from depression. Jesus used this same basic concept when comforting His deeply depressed disciples on the eve of His departure (John 14:16, 18-19).

Jesus' favorite word for His promised presence in the Holy Spirit is *paraclete*—"the One called alongside." Engrave Jesus' words on your mind until they are such a part of you that, during your lowest depression, regardless of how you feel, you will know that He is with you.

REFLECTION

Which of the above suggestions has helped you deal with depression in the past? Which suggestion might you try in the future? In what ways can you thank "the One called alongside" for His abiding presence in your life?

Healing Prayer

"The prayer of a righteous man is powerful and effective."   *(James 5:16b)*

Many of us need healing for childhood and teenage memories. However, many times the painful memory is more recent, a part of adult life. This is especially true of some of the traumas surrounding our modern tragedies involving sex, violence, and the sense of betrayal in a divorce. The same principles apply and bring about release and healing when often the more ordinary means of prayer do not. The best biblical example of this is the way Jesus handled Peter's denial and restoration.

John 18:18 and 21:9 are the only two places in the New Testament where the word for "a charcoal fire" is used. Surely this is more than coincidence. It is obvious that Jesus deliberately set the stage for His conversation with Peter on the beach that post-Resurrection morning. Peter had denied Him three times while standing near a charcoal fire in the high priest's courtyard. Now he would be asked to affirm his love and loyalty three times. Everyone knows this part, but the fact that Jesus staged the conversation by asking Peter to relive the very setting of his denial seems to be overlooked. Surely the memory of those courtyard coals had been burning like fire in the conscience and memory of Peter.

Here the Master Psychiatrist led Peter to face his most traumatic memory, and used a charcoal fire to cauterize and heal Peter's pain and shame. With the sting removed, Peter would be able to use that burning memory not as a curse which crippled, but as a spark to ignite him to an even deeper devotion, even unto death!

I know this may all sound much too simple—like a shortcut. It is not meant to be a cure-all, for this type of healing prayer doesn't apply to everybody. However, it does apply to some. The difference is perhaps largely a difference of degree in our lives. I am trusting the Holy Spirit will apply it to those who need this deeper kind of healing experience.

R E F L E C T I O N

What are some memories that you need to relive in order to find healing? Identify a person in whom you have confidence, who really knows how to pray, and with whom you can share your deepest, most painful memories.

Frozen People

"There is a time for everything . . . a time to weep and a time to laugh, a time to mourn and a time to dance."
(Ecclesiastes 3:1, 4)

Brave boys don't cry." This childhood slogan takes several unhelpful forms: "Children are to be seen and not heard," or, "If you don't stop crying, I'll give you something to cry about!" Our cultural overemphasis on certain sports, the adulation of the "strong, silent person," and the inference that if one expresses emotions he or she is weak—all add strength to this destructive motto.

Some of us had this deadly childhood slogan so woven into our lives that as adults we are simply not able to express our real feelings. If feelings do surface, we don't know how to handle them. We feel ashamed or afraid or dirty or weak—whether we express them or not.

I believe it is best to counter this destructive motto by considering the emotional life of Jesus and seeing what part feelings played in His life and just exactly how He handled them. I am so glad that Jesus was literally one of us. In fact, He was far more human in regard to His emotions than many evangelical Christians. For many of us have been badly misled by the combination of a Puritan and more recent *macho* tradition. We feel it may be all right for a woman to express her emotions, but not a man.

And the attitude carries over into the Christian life.

To be a really victorious Christian means we should never be grieved or upset, sorrowful or angry, or moved much by anything. We have falsely made a "great-stone-face," expressionless, highly controlled, unemotional stoicism the prime evidence of being an overcoming Christian.

If Jesus is our pattern, then this is a grotesque, distorted image to put before people as an ideal. Because these standards are false, they are unreachable, and yet many sincere Christians try to reach them and experience a great deal of unnecessary guilt in the process. Jesus was never afraid to express His emotions, never ashamed to let people see and know how He really felt. Instead of being God's stoic people, we can become His holy and wholesome children.

R E F L E C T I O N

Do you find it difficult to express your real feelings? Why or why not? What are some times when you have been afraid or ashamed to express your emotions?

How Far
Is Too Far?

"The body is not meant for sexual immorality, but for the Lord, and the Lord for the body."

(1 Corinthians 6:13b)

I f you are single and in a dating relationship, your Master has given you the responsibility of protecting the sexual purity of the person you are dating. He or she has been entrusted to your care. This principle will help answer a question Christian couples ask: "How far should we go?"

Many a young person has assured me, "I am able to control my sex desires, and I know when to quit." That's only half of the answer! The more important half is in regard to your partner. Is what you do or want to do with that person something which will help or hinder them in maintaining control? *Each one is responsible for helping the other maintain sexual purity.*

This moral principle is at the very heart of loyalty and faithfulness in marriage. To commit adultery is to break the commitment and to betray the trust of the partner God has put into your care. It is also moral "breaking and entering," stealing what does not belong to you as well as failing to protect what does.

A dear friend of mine was spiritually mature beyond his years and a gifted preacher. As a young pastor in his late twenties, he was often invited to speak at youth camps, retreats, and revival services in churches. On one such occasion he was conducting a special series of meetings for a church in a distant city.

He had been staying in the spacious home of a wealthy church family. Late one night he was awakened by Jackie, the beautiful eighteen-year-old daughter of the family. She said she had fallen in love with him and wanted to have sex with him. Gently, but firmly, he talked her out of it. She returned to her own bedroom embarrassed and in tears.

Seven years later he received a note, the kind one receives from a bride in appreciation for a wedding present. Puzzled, he checked with his wife who confirmed that no gift had been sent. They thought it was a mistake until another tiny note fell out of its folds. It was from Jackie, warmly thanking him for giving her the most valuable wedding gift she had received—her virginity!

R E F L E C T I O N

What kinds of struggles have you had with sexual purity? In what ways can you help your spouse, family, and friends to maintain sexual purity?

The Sure Road to Maturity

"Taste and see that the Lord is good; blessed is the man who takes refuge in Him."

(Psalm 34:8)

The surest way to become a defeated, morbid, unstable Christian is to always ask yourself, "Well, how do I feel?" To base your relationship to God on the condition of your feelings is a certain sign of spiritual babyhood. The sure road to maturity is to learn to live above moods and feelings. This is going to require discipline. And it will require particular effort for feeling-centered individuals who have never learned in other areas of life to seek truth before feeling.

I like the suggestion which comes to us from our dear missionary friend from India, Sister Anna Mow. She gives her formula for those blue days when you feel depressed and condemned, and are prone to doubt your salvation because you just feel so bad. On those blue days, Anna Mow talks to herself. And that's a good idea. I do that occasionally too, simply because I enjoy intelligent conversation! This is what Anna says to herself when she is not feeling good:

- ❖ Did I get enough sleep last night?
- ❖ Have I hurt someone, intentionally or inadvertently?
- ❖ Do I feel resentment or self-pity?

If all is well in these three areas and Anna can find no

reason for her spiritual indigestion, she just throws back her head and laughs at herself. And what a wonderfully contagious laugh she has, as she says to herself, "All right, Anna Mow, you stay here in the blues if you want to. I'm going on with the Lord."

There is a profound truth in Anna Mow's simple formula. You are not just your feelings. At any given moment you are greater than the sum total of your thoughts and feelings. Your selfhood is above and beyond any feelings you may be having, and you can transcend your feelings. One of the most important steps of growth in the Christian life is to reach the place where you affirm this truth about yourself.

R E F L E C T I O N

What are some times when you have based your relationship to God on the condition of your feelings? Are there times when you feel so blue that you doubt your own salvation? What are some things you can do to cope with your feelings?

Emotional Vitamins

"Whoever welcomes one of these little children in My name welcomes Me; and whoever welcomes Me does not welcome Me but the One who sent Me."
(Mark 9:37)

Friends described Jack as one who "had it all together." Successful in his work, happily married with an attractive family, he was well respected in both church and community. Then when he hit thirty-five things began to change. It was the emergence of negative and destructive emotions that had pushed Jack out of his comfortable life and led him to seek help.

At first Jack was embarrassed and puzzled.

"All hell seems to have broken loose in my personality," he hesitantly confessed to me. When we surveyed possible physical and situational factors, we came up with none. Slowly it became clear—Jack seemed gripped with deep feelings of fear, insecurity, and self-doubt. In spite of all the successful realities to the contrary, he had an overwhelming sense he was a complete failure. This was so strong that he was also being tempted by certain desires and sins quite new to him, which added to a sense of spiritual failure.

From his earliest years Jack felt he was neither wanted nor loved by his parents, particularly his father. Jack fought back the hurt and tears as he shared a kaleidoscope of recurring painful scenes. One especially haunted him. He was only in kindergarten, and his mother was bringing him home from the hospital after some minor surgery. He felt nauseated and weak as she helped him into the house. Dad was working on the car, his head down under the hood. Without even looking up, he had said in a disgusted tone, "All right now, don't come sniveling around me. I've got important work to do."

Jack had never received the life-giving nourishment of parental grace—Acceptance, Affection, and Affirmation. Now he was suffering from a case of "emotional vitamin A deficiency." There was a huge hole at the center of Jack's being and it was disrupting his relationship with God.

Like Jack, you may have God and your parents all tangled up together. It will take time to get them separated, but take hope—this reconstruction will help you have a God fit to love and to live with.

R E F L E C T I O N

In what ways has your self-concept suffered as a result of neglect, conditional acceptance, or unpredictable affection during your developmental years?

Cut the Cord

"And when you stand praying, if you hold anything against anyone, forgive him."

(Mark 11:25a)

Though a really fine Christian who contributed to many areas of church life, Arlene devalued her spiritual life. Much of our counseling had centered on her mother, a deeply religious woman, a leader in her denomination, but whose overcritical and perfectionistic ways had poured out as a constant stream over Arlene. As the hurts and humiliations surfaced, so did a heavy layer of resentment she had never faced.

One day she was expressing it so realistically that I said to her, "It sure looks to me like you need to cut the umbilical cord to your mother, and stop letting her feed you with those downgrading evaluations." Arlene looked a bit startled. "Oh, I'm sorry," she said, "I guess I didn't make it plain. My mother's been dead for over five years now."

I was embarrassed and mumbled out an apology. I noticed Arlene clammed up for the rest of the session, so inwardly I was thinking, *Boy, Seamands, you sure blew it today!*

When she came back the next time she said to me, "I realize you know I'm a nurse, but do you know where I do most of my work?"

"No, I'm afraid I don't."

"Well, I spend most of my time helping deliver babies.

I suppose I've assisted doctors in cutting the umbilical cord hundreds of times. So last week when you said I needed to cut the umbilical cord to my mother, it really shocked me. As I drove home, the only thing I could picture in my mind was a cord stretching from here right into my mother's grave down in Florida! I actually dreamed about that crazy cord twice. You were exactly right. This week I spent a lot of time in prayer, and I found the grace to forgive her, and to ask God to forgive me for resenting and blaming her all these years. And I've been amazed—I'm not feeding on her wretched evaluations of me anymore. I am beginning to get a whole new sense of who I am as God's daughter, and I'm learning to feed on His opinions of me. And it's beginning to feel awfully good!"

Hate keeps us chained to the people and the pains of the past. Only forgiveness and love can free us!

R E F L E C T I O N

Do you need to "cut the cord" to anyone? Are you feeding on God's opinion of you? Why or why not?

The Revolution

"Humble yourselves before the Lord, and He will lift you up." *(James 4:10)*

Again and again I am asked, "But how is it possible for a truly born-again and Spirit-filled Christian to continue suffering from unhealthy patterns of meeting life and its needs?"

Paul Tournier in his great book *The Person Reborn* explains it so clearly in a parable. He says that a Christian experience is like a revolution. A new prince has taken over a country by means of a coup d'état. Among the crowd that acclaims him are the followers of the fallen monarch who is now powerless. For the moment they seem to be the most zealous partisans of the new ruler. But their change of heart is not sincere, for they are the enemy who will secretly scheme the gradual undermining of the new regime. If the reigning prince wins some triumph they bow down and pretend to submit, only to raise their heads once again at the first opportunity to undermine his power.

Tournier says that this is what happens in the case of some of the deeply submerged elements in our mental make-up. They hide themselves and share in the victory we feel. But they have not capitulated and they may later succeed in sabotaging those victories if we do not unmask them. The process of unmasking them, he says, is a slow one and may require the help of medicine, psychiatry, and spiritual power.

This is an effective illustration of how a person can be a very genuine Christian and still have certain emotional conflicts and complexes which need the gradual healing and work of the Holy Spirit. Let us consider our crisis Christian experience as the moment of revolution when the New Prince takes over; and then let us look at the growth in Christlikeness and in emotional maturity as the process whereby every part of our personality is brought under the total lordship of our Prince and Lord—Jesus Christ!

R E F L E C T I O N
What unhealthy coping mechanisms have you used to get your needs met? What, if any, parts of your personality need to be brought under the lordship of Jesus Christ?

Reconciled

"He has committed us to the message of reconciliation."
(2 Corinthians 5:19b)

Some years back, at the request of a member of my church, I visited a woman in the Intensive Care Unit of the hospital. When I introduced myself she said, "Reverend, I've been trying to pray, but it's no use. I don't know the Bible, and I've not been to church in thirty years. I know God won't listen to me. I've just been too bad."

I asked her if she wanted to tell me about it. I leaned closer as she told me a sad story. When she was a teenager her mother, whom she loved deeply, suddenly died. She was overwhelmed with grief, and the night after the funeral she and her older brother went out and got "roaring drunk." With great shame, she whispered to me how in their drunken stupor they had slept together.

"That's why it's no use for me to pray. I know God can't forgive me, since I sure can't forgive myself."

In our devotions that very morning, Helen and I had read from 2 Corinthians 5:19-20. It was fresh in my memory that I was God's personal ambassador with His authority. I took her by the hand and said, "Rosie, my name is David. And I want you to know that God Himself personally sent me to tell you that Jesus died on the cross for you, and that He forgives you for that sin and all the rest of your sins." We talked a little longer and prayed together. Her last words to me were, "What you said God told you to tell me was wonderful. I'm going to try and believe it."

I returned the next morning to see Rosie, but her bed was empty. The nurse recognized me and said, "She died in the night. But she told me to give you a message. 'Tell that Reverend David that I *did* pray, and I *did* believe what God told me, and I've got peace in my heart, and everything between me and God is all right!' "

Second Corinthians 5:19 says: "God was reconciling the world to Himself in Christ, not counting men's sins against them." But I like Rosie's translation, "I believed. . .and everything between me and God is all right!"

R E F L E C T I O N

Do you believe God's personal message to you—that your sins are forgiven? In what ways might forgiving yourself be linked to experiencing God's grace?

GRACE IS GOD'S

LOVE IN ACTION

TOWARD THOSE WHO

DO NOT DESERVE IT.

An Imagineer
for God

"I press on to take hold of that for which Christ Jesus took hold of me. . . . Forgetting what is behind and straining toward what is ahead, I press on toward the goal to win the prize for which God has called me heavenward in Christ Jesus."

(Philippians 3:12b-14)

God does not work dramatically in everyone's life. But I believe He wants to give to all of His redeemed children some kind of a dream and vision which will hold them steadily on His intended course for their lives.

Many years ago, a young university student in England was asked to go to India and fill a job for just one year. This seemed to be an interesting possibility so he accepted the offer. While he was there he felt challenged by the work, and the dream of a lifetime of service began to fill his mind.

To make a long story short, Lesslie Newbigin became one of South India's most prominent evangelical missionaries. His books on missions and theology are classics. Newbigin had such an outstanding record that when several denominations united to form the indigenous Church of South India, he was one of the very few missionaries to be elected Bishop.

Let's make it personal. Do you have a dream? Have you ever had one? Perhaps I should ask if you still have the dream you once had—that high and holy vision for your life? A godly picture of who God intends you to be which propels you toward the goal? Which compels you to give your all? A dream like this is a form of sanctified imagination holding before us an inner video of all we're meant to be.

Richard Baxter, the great Puritan divine, had a way with words. He took two common words, *imagination* and *engineer* and said that every Christian ought to be an *imagineer* for God. Such a dream gives us an inner power, a force which drives us to "press on toward the goal."

R E F L E C T I O N

How would you respond to the questions regarding the dream God has for your life? Are you an "imagineer" for God? Why or why not?

Our Most
Common Failure

"The law was added so that the trespass might increase. But where sin increased, grace increased all the more, so that, just as sin reigned in death, so also grace might reign through righteousness to bring eternal life through Jesus Christ our Lord."
(Romans 5:20-21)

On September 8, 1974, stuntman Evel Knievel attempted to vault Idaho's Snake River Canyon. Prior to this Knievel had achieved notoriety with his stunt riding on motorcycles. He would take off from a wooden ramp and at very high speeds sail across snarls of live rattlesnakes or lines of parked cars. He was seriously injured several times and boasted he had broken every major bone in his body except his neck. This attempt to rocket across a fearsome chasm was his most daring feat.

On that day he flashed a check for $6 million, purportedly his advance fee from the anticipated 200,000 spectators and the closed-circuit TV receipts. Actually only a few motorcycle gangs and about 15,000 people gathered at Twin Falls to watch him soar across the canyon. But his Sky Cycle never made it. Fortunately for him, the landing parachute enabled it to drift down to the river's edge. Rescue helicopters brought him back up, bruised and humiliated but not seriously injured. The 1975 *Encyclopedia Britannica Yearbook* aptly described it as "the year's most spectacular failure!"

Actually, it is a vivid illustration of humankind's most common failure—a prideful and evil attempt to cross the moral chasm and "become as God." It is doomed to failure, for Scripture assures us there's no way to make it. Because we are fallen beings, we lack the power and will always fall short. And no matter how hard or how many times we try, we will always come up short and fall again. It is indeed a vicious cycle and there's no way to break out of it in our own strength.

Thank God, there is a better way—His way. God's gracious provision for bridging the canyon, the way of grace is the only answer.

R EFLECTION

What are some ways that you have tried to "become as God" in your life or the lives of others? In what ways does pride interfere with your relationship with God?

A Lack of Communication

"Speaking the truth in love, we will in all things grow up into Him who is the Head, that is, Christ."
(Ephesians 4:15)

The greatest problem in relationships, especially marriage, is communication. Fortunately for us, Paul defined mature communication in Ephesians 4:14-15. Paul was 2,000 years ahead of the times in his basic communication principles. "Speaking the truth in love" is mature Christian communication.

The greatest cause of unhappiness in marriage is the inability of spouses to communicate openly and lovingly with one another. All too often marital communication is still on a childish level.

How do children communicate? Some speak the truth all right, but they are cruel, sharp, and hurtful. Then there are children who cannot speak the truth. They are too afraid of their feelings to express them. Maybe every time they did express their feelings, they were not allowed to continue. Or perhaps they have never seen or heard a true expression of feelings from the people they live with.

"Speaking the truth in love" is a learned art. Maybe I ought to say it is an unlearned art, because often we first have to unlearn things that our homes and life experiences and our sick culture have taught us. Sometimes in agony and sweat and tears, we have to put them off and change our whole way of communicating.

Isn't it incredible that a married couple can love each other, live together, make love to one another, bring up children together, yet never really communicate to one another what they are actually feeling? By failing to say what is really wrong, they express in other unsanctified ways their displeasure, their disagreement, and their anger.

Gibson Winter reminds us that conflict is always the price of deepening intimacy between persons and can only be resolved by proper communication. "When I grew up," said Paul, "I put away childish ways of communicating; I learned to speak the truth in love." That will mean confrontation, and conflict which is ultimately creative and helpful. It will result in resolving the conflict and thus deepening our love.

R E F L E C T I O N

In communicating with others, do you find yourself either not speaking the truth, or not speaking in love? How has poor communication affected intimacy in your relationships with others?

Back to the Father's House

"But while he was still a long way off, his father saw him and was filled with compassion for him; he ran to his son, threw his arms around him and kissed him."
(Luke 15:20)

Back in the early 1970s, a young man named Andy came to me for help. He had reached the end of his rope, was in a deep depression, and had been contemplating suicide. As I sat and listened to his story I couldn't help thinking of Jesus' Parable of the Prodigal. In my mind I followed the parallel at every step.

Andy had run away from a good home, gotten into heavy drugs, and begun to lose control of his drinking. Prior to his enrollment at Asbury College he had been living in a commune in an eastern city. The three fellows and two girls shared everything—lodging, food, and sex. But life had fallen apart. Now he was empty and fed up.

Before I realized what I was saying I blurted out, "You know, Andy, you've done everything the Prodigal did except eat the pigs' food."

He looked startled and fell silent. I started to apologize, but the Holy Spirit was way ahead of me.

"Oh no," he said, "I just remembered. . .I've even done that! I attended the Woodstock Rock Festival in 1969. The crowd was so huge [over 400,000] that they ran out of food, and we ended up almost starving. But no one could get out to buy food. So finally helicopters flew over and dropped macrobiotic hog food in huge bundles.

And we all grabbed it and ate it with our bare hands."
Andy groaned as he remembered the taste.

After that there was only one incident of the parable left for Andy to make the parallel complete—the journey back to the Father's house. Before long that part of the story had also been fulfilled! Thank God for His steadfast love and His faithful grace which reaches into every human situation.

R E F L E C T I O N

In what ways does your life story parallel the Parable of the Prodigal Son? Have you made the journey back to the Father's house? Why or why not?

The Tinker

"The Spirit helps us in our weakness. We do not know what we ought to pray for, but the Spirit Himself intercedes for us with groans that words cannot express."
(Romans 8:26)

Have you ever heard the story of Henry Ford and Charlie Steinmetz? Steinmetz was a dwarf, ugly and deformed, but he had one of the greatest minds in the field of electricity that the world has ever known. Steinmetz built the great generators for Henry Ford in his first plant in Dearborn, Michigan.

One day those generators broke down and the plant came to a halt. They brought in ordinary mechanics and helpers who couldn't get the generators going again. They were losing money. Then Ford called Steinmetz. The genius came, seemed to just putter around for a few hours, and then threw the switch that put the great Ford plant back into operation.

A few days later Henry Ford received a bill from Steinmetz for $10,000. Although Ford was a very rich man, he returned the bill with a note, "Charlie, isn't this bill just a little high for a few hours of tinkering around on those motors?"

Steinmetz returned the bill to Ford. This time it read: "For tinkering around on those motors: $10. For knowing where to tinker: $9,990. Total: $10,000."

Henry Ford paid the bill.

The Holy Spirit knows where to tinker. We do not know what we ought to be praying for. We often do not receive, because we ask for the wrong things. As we look for healing, we need to ask the Holy Spirit to show us what we need to know about ourselves, and then to guide us in our prayers.

R E F L E C T I O N

How are you feeling right now about letting the Holy Spirit "tinker" in your life at an emotional level? Try to put your response in the form of a short sentence prayer to God.

Enough Faith

"Be joyful in hope, patient in affliction, faithful in prayer."   *(Romans 12:12)*

After many weeks of counseling a young man, it was obvious that he had reached a point of decision. The risk of giving up all his old ways really frightened him. He said he was "trying hard to believe" that he could be changed, but wasn't making much progress in that direction. As he was about to leave, I said almost offhandedly, "Don't worry, Tom, I've got enough faith for both of us." It didn't seem to register, for he made no reply and I didn't observe a flicker of hope in his expression.

That afternoon he was to meet with a bunch of guys in a small prayer group. He felt so discouraged that he almost didn't go, but at the last minute decided to attend. He shared his discouragement about that day's counseling session. It must have been God's Spirit at work, because one of the other fellows commented, also quite casually, "Hey, Tom, don't worry about it. We've got enough faith for all of us, including you!"

Somehow God used the "coincidence" of the two statements to turn on a tiny pilot light in his heart. That in turn ignited a small flame of faith which started to burn brighter. Before that meeting was over, Tom, to use John Wesley's oft-quoted words, "felt his heart strangely warmed." That turned out to be the crucial beginning of a changed life.

Yes, the miracles of resurrection and release continue in people's lives even today, if we will believe *Him,* and if we will unbind *them.*

R E F L E C T I O N

When was the last time someone had enough faith to support you through a difficult time in your life? When was the last time you supported someone else?

No Special Immunity

"Did I not tell you that if you believed, you would see the glory of God?" *(John 11:40)*

L ord, the one You love is sick." This was the message sent from Mary and Martha to Jesus when their brother Lazarus fell ill.

I sense a complaint as well as a request in their words. It's a subtle, perhaps unconscious, expression of an age-old mystery, "Lord, we thought that You loved him; how has this happened to him?"

Do you remember times when your bewildered heart sent a similar message to the Lord? How well I remember such a day back in 1948. Our first son, healthy, ten-month-old David, had been cut down by fulminant bacillary dysentery in a matter of hours. We were told later that *fulminant* meant "to strike like lightning," and that certainly was accurate. We buried him in the reddish soil of Bidar the next morning. Dear Indian friends and fellow missionaries streamed through our home for several days. My parents and brother were with us too. But after a few days we were all alone. Night came, and our three-year-old daughter, disturbed by the disappearance of her little brother, had finally gone to sleep. The empty silence was deafening. The single hurricane lantern cast eerie shadows on the walls as Helen began playing the piano and we began to sing one of our favorite hymns, "Spirit of God, Descend Upon My Heart." We did fine until the words of the fourth stanza seemed to jump out and gnaw at something deep within us.

> Teach me to feel that Thou art always nigh;
> Teach me the struggles of the soul to bear,
> To check the rising doubt, the rebel sigh;
> Teach me the patience of unanswered prayer.

All at once my voice broke and I began to fight back the tears. Unwanted and unwelcome thoughts which I had pushed down suddenly erupted within me and spilled out into a bitter dialogue with God.

"Lord, I don't understand. We left home and family and friends and came 10,000 miles to serve You as missionaries in India. We love You and we believe that You love us. How could You have let this happen to us? Why?"

In the coming days, God had to teach both of us more about life and death, love and suffering. One of those lessons was that Jesus never promises us a special immunity from tragedies, hurts, and pains, but He does promise a special immanence—His *presence*.

R E F L E C T I O N

In what ways have you struggled with the issue of desiring God's immunity from tragedies? How is the promise of Jesus' presence comforting?

The Treadmill

*"For it is by grace you have been saved, through faith—
and this not from yourselves, it is the gift of God."*
(Ephesians 2:8)

Devadas was a thorough student of the Scriptures and a faithful witness among his Hindu colleagues. If necessary, Devadas would have died *for* his Christianity. The real question was why he seemed to be almost dying *from* it.

For well over an hour, he shared his never-ending battle with guilt, anxiety, low self-esteem, denial and repression of emotions such as anger or depression, and a legalism resulting from a damaged, oversensitive conscience. It seemed obvious to me that Devadas just wasn't as *spiritual* as he ought to be. So I began to counsel him the only way I knew—a one-to-one preaching session.

However, to all of my sincere questions with their implied and well-meaning suggestions, he kept giving me answers that just didn't fit my simplistic solutions.

"Pastor, I have increased my time in the Scriptures as well as my prayer time. But to be perfectly honest with you, neither of these have helped much. In fact, as strange as it may sound, I seem to be somewhat worse. Something inside keeps telling me I *ought* to read even more, and I *should* pray even more. I cannot understand it, but I never seem to be able to do quite enough. In fact, that's what seems to be the whole problem."

I was stumped. Somewhere in the midst of my frustration, the Holy Spirit strongly suggested, "Why don't you just shut up and listen carefully to what he is saying? You've been so anxious to impress him with your answers that you haven't really heard his questions."

For the first time, I actually heard the meaning of what he was saying. More important still, I began to *feel* his pain. *"I feel like I ought to do more."* From that heart-to-heart encounter, there emerged the hazy beginnings of my ministry to many hurting and disheartened Christians who were trapped on the treadmill of spiritual performance, with no way to get off.

R E F L E C T I O N

Do you ever feel as if you are on a treadmill of spiritual performance? Why or why not? Have you ever been so anxious to share answers with a troubled friend that you neglected to listen?

Watch and Pray

"Watch and pray so that you will not fall into temptation."   *(Matthew 26:41a)*

Verbal, physical, and sexual abuse marked Evelyn's youth. A teenage marriage had only created more problems. Soon this young divorcee was trying to fill an almost insatiable need for male attention and love by going from one affair to another.

And then, a Christian coworker introduced her to a warm, loving fellowship group, and she was dramatically converted. It was while a student in college that she came for counseling. In addition to the wounds of her early years, some of her own past sins had left deep scars on her life. Slowly but surely, God's grace brought remarkable changes to Evelyn's personality. The one area where she knew she must "watch and pray" the most was about her almost compulsive need for men.

Evelyn graduated, got a job as a secretary, and because she was conscientious and hard-working, climbed the ladder to personal assistant to the head of the company. This meant many hours spent together. Although he was married with a family, she felt herself being emotionally drawn to him.

One day, when he asked her to accompany him on a business trip, she knew down deep in her heart what this meant. She prayed and wept about it before God, but that old emptiness seemed to be drawing her into a vortex from which she couldn't escape.

On their second night away, her boss expressed his feelings for her and invited her to his room after the business sessions were over. She accepted his invitation but, during the evening session, a terrific struggle took place in her. Evelyn described it as a tug-of-war with her as the rope! As she and her boss walked out of the meeting, she stopped and said:

> Jim, I admire you more than any man I know. I want to be with you tonight so much I'm actually aching. It's my fault for leading you on. Forgive me. But during the meeting I remembered that a man from Kentucky told me how much God loved me, and I believed him. And I just can't go against that kind of love. It's done too much for my life and means too much to me.

Evelyn had found the secret—the realization of God's unconditional love and undeserved grace that holds us steady in temptation. Not guilt and self-condemnation, but grace and its accompanying sense of self-worth.

R E F L E C T I O N

What holds you steady in temptation? What tug-of-war takes place inside you?

Delays and Detours

"Our fathers disciplined us for a little while as they thought best; but God disciplines us for our good, that we may share in His holiness."

(Hebrews 12:10)

Following our time in Bombay, Helen and I were still uncertain about our missionary service. We went for a short time to another rural mission station where it was thought I would return to my evangelistic work. Unfortunately, it was during the monsoon season and that year brought record-breaking rains. My four-wheel-drive Jeep could hardly get out of the driveway, let alone navigate the impassable village roads.

One day as I sat looking out the office window watching it rain, I felt as if I were in a dungeon of darkness, distress, despair, disappointment, and delay all wrapped into one humid, wet blanket. Deep in my soul I began another one of my arguments with God. *Didn't He realize what all this was doing to me? Me—David Seamands, unable to do anything. All my many talents being wasted in this overgrown, muddy village.*

And as clear as crystal the inner voice of the Spirit said to me, "David, keep the division of labor straight. If it's My will that you spend the rest of your life in this overgrown, muddy village, then that's My business, not yours. Your part in all this is to dig down and go as deep as you can. That's your business. You take care of the depth, and I'll take care of the length and the breadth."

I cannot explain it, but something inside me clicked back into place. It was God's way of restoring and refashioning my dream.

It rained for the next two months, producing serious floods in an otherwise dry area. During that time, in addition to studying the Bible, I read fifty books. I digested them and filed their contents, and God gave me a lot of wonderful ideas which I was going to need in the days to come. For in a short time we were sent to a large, inner-city pastorate in Bangalore where we spent six years. Then back to the States to Wilmore, Kentucky and Asbury College and Seminary. We did not know that God was going to change the entire course of our lives as well as the contents of our dream. But now we understand it was all an important part of His discipline of delay and detour.

REFLECTION

What kinds of arguments do you have with God? In what ways have you experienced God's discipline of delay or detour when it comes to your dreams and plans for the future?

Experiencing Grief

"When Jesus heard what had happened, He withdrew by boat privately to a solitary place."
(Matthew 14:13a)

A few years ago some English archaeologists, digging in the sands of Egypt, found a tomb inside a cave which had been sealed for almost 4,000 years. On the outside of a beautiful carved stone coffin was the name of a little girl. As they were about to open the sarcophagus, they discovered another inscription. It said, "O my life, my love, my little one, would God I had died for thee!" The two men looked at each other and once again sealed the cave. They were so moved by what they saw they just couldn't bear to intrude into the privacy of those heartbroken parents.

Grief over the death of someone you love is one of life's strongest emotions. What should be our reaction to this universal human experience? How did Jesus handle grief and sorrow?

We can find one clue in Jesus' reaction when they brought Him the news that John the Baptist, His own cousin whom He admired so deeply, had been beheaded. We are told that Jesus withdrew to a lonely place by Himself. When the bad news first comes, don't we all want to get away from people and be by ourselves? It's not necessarily self-pity or escapism. It's a natural first response to sorrow. Sometime later, Jesus called His disciples aside from the crowds to be by themselves, and later went by Himself to pray (Matthew 14:22-23).

Here is a beautiful pattern we can all follow: withdrawal for a while, but not for too long. For if we grieve too long by ourselves, we may lose our sense of balance and perspective and find we are grieving not over someone we have lost, but for ourselves. So the next thing to do is to get with our closest friends. And certainly to pray, to spend time with the great Comforter.

These are the proper ways to handle grief. We never need to be ashamed to admit our sorrow and to express it openly.

R E F L E C T I O N

When faced with grief, do you ever feel ashamed about weeping, withdrawing, or getting help from your closest friends? What prevents you from seeing these ways of handling grief as natural and normal, human and helpful?

God's Inner Cruise Control

"He makes me lie down in green pastures, He leads me beside quiet waters, He restores my soul."
(Psalm 23:2-3)

We all have physical limitations, and we need to stay within them. Occasionally, we all are called on to go without sufficient rest; we have reserves on which we can draw. But to make the exception the rule means you will live regularly with fatigue. If you do so, I can guarantee that you will suffer from chronic, and perhaps even clinical and pathological depression. You will feel like the man who said he not only had an identity crisis, but also an energy crisis. He didn't know who he was and he was just too tired to find out!

Let me make it clear that it makes no difference if you are in the Lord's service! God does not suspend His laws and make cosmic pets of preachers, missionaries, high achievers, and overcommitted church workers. They still come under the laws He has built into our bodies and emotions. And you cannot regularly violate those laws and expect to get by with it.

What kind of load are you carrying? When was the last time you had a thorough physical examination? How about a dental checkup? Are you getting regular physical exercise? Are you eating properly and regularly?

My niece, who is a doctor, at one time specialized in emergency-room treatment. I asked her what she did with depressed people who had attempted suicide.

"Well, sometimes the first thing we do is to feed them, often a steak dinner. They are generally low in protein. We often discover that they have not eaten properly for two or three days. When their protein level is very low, their energy level is low, and their depression level is high." There are Christians who consistently neglect the physical area of their lives and then wonder why they are depressed.

Did you ever think that perhaps your depression is God's built-in cruise control for your life? Trying to slow you down, trying to balance out your emotions, because you regularly try to live above realistic possibilities?

R E F L E C T I O N

Do a quick personal inventory, noting any areas where you may be living beyond your physical means. What, if anything, keeps you from maintaining your physical well-being?

The Feeler of Our Humiliation

"God has poured out His love into our hearts by the Holy Spirit."   *(Romans 5:5b)*

How can I ever forget the young woman in her thirties who kept sobbing out her story of being sexually molested by an uncle.

"I was only a little girl then and I cried out to God every time it happened, but God didn't stop him. You keep talking about a God of love, but I can't believe it. You're asking me to trust Him now, but how can I when He didn't hear me then?"

During one of our weekend seminars, this incest victim expressed her deep resentment against God—and me—for even daring to suggest she needed to forgive the one she blamed for ruining her life. A bitter spirit had poisoned her relationships, especially with men, and she felt that her tragedy gave her every "right" to be resentful.

At the close of a morning session, this woman came to the altar for a special time of healing prayer. I wondered what possible word from the cross God could speak to a victim of sexual abuse. The word came when the young woman heard that in the earliest paintings of the Crucifixion, Jesus was always naked. Thus Christ, in His humiliation and disgrace, had identified with all victims of the shame of nakedness. It began to dawn on her that Jesus understood the pain of shameful exposure, because He had been through it Himself. Therefore, Jesus was not judging or condemning her anger against God, but was weeping with her and for her. Her hateful spirit melted away as God "poured out His love" into her heart "by the Holy Spirit" (Romans 5:5).

I had never realized this aspect of Christ's passion until I asked Corrie ten Boom what was the worst thing she had suffered in the German concentration camps during the Holocaust. She paused and replied, "It was the nakedness, so often having to be naked before all those jeering soldiers. That was the worst of all!" Yes, humiliation was part of our Lord's total identification with the world's suffering.

R E F L E C T I O N

Do you have any sexual attitudes or behavior that might be distorted as a result of sexual abuse? What are some ways that Jesus has identified with your sufferings, particularly any humiliating events?

God-Bonded

"I have put my hope in Your word."
(Psalm 119:74b)

D r. Ken Magid is a practicing clinical psychologist and professor who teaches physicians in a medical school. He has written a book called *High Risk: Children Without Conscience.* His main thesis is that America is in a "bonding crisis." This means that we are raising a whole generation of children who are victims of "the unattached child syndrome." They have never been truly "bonded" with their parents and, unless this is healed and changed, they will never get close to anyone. Because of parental behavior, he feels these children will grow into adults who do not seem to have a conscience and who are unable to genuinely relate to other people.

Dr. Magid describes them as "trust bandits," the con artists of society, pathological liars, and in some instances dangerous criminals. At the core of their lives is a deep-seated rage born of their unfulfilled needs. It seems to be locked in their souls because of the emotional abandonment they experienced as children. Dr. Magid says it's as if a voice inside them says, "I trusted you to be there and to take care of me and you weren't. It hurts so much that I will not trust anyone, ever. I must control everything—and everybody—to ward off being abandoned again." His book is filled with illustrations of many such persons so badly damaged by their homes that they have a difficult time ever receiving or giving love to others.

I am glad that we can have a more optimistic viewpoint because of the transforming power of Christ. Truly, "hope does not disappoint us, because God has poured out His love into our hearts by the Holy Spirit, whom He has given us" (Romans 5:5). For those who are badly scarred by the kind of damage Dr. Magid describes, deep healing grace is available to bring wholeness into their relationships with others.

R E F L E C T I O N
Have you ever had a difficult time receiving or giving love to others? In what ways do you think your home life has affected your ability to have healthy relationships?

GOD IS THE GREAT

ALCHEMIST WHO CAN

TAKE EVERY HURT

AND TURN IT INTO

SPIRITUAL GOLD.

The Ultimate
Crisis of Life

---

*"If anyone would come after Me, he must deny himself
and take up his cross and follow Me."*
                                        (Mark 8:34b)

One of the mistakes in our philosophy of holiness
and sanctification is to ask people to do something that is psychologically and emotionally
impossible: namely, to move too quickly from conversion
to self-surrender. It seems that God has to bring most of
us through a series of steps until we arrive at total desperation.

It took me four years to get from "here to there." In
the battlefield of my spiritual life, I surrendered many
attachments, many relationships, many ambitions. I was
healed of many hangups and damaged emotions. I
answered the call to preach and to go to the mission
field. But I hung on to my self until the Spirit in His gracious work, largely through the reading of Oswald
Chambers' book, *My Utmost for His Highest,* took the
veil from my eyes. One lonely summer as a student at
Asbury College I saw it, but I didn't realize what had happened until three weeks later. One miserable July night
on the third floor of Morrison dormitory, I saw myself as I
never had before: I saw all of its loathsomeness, its
deceptiveness, its rebelliousness.

You see, before my conversion I felt convicted as a
guilty criminal who had broken God's laws. But now I felt
a different conviction—as if I were guilty of treason

against the state, that I had within me an unyielded being that questioned the very right and rulership of God Himself. One statement of Chambers kept hammering at my heart: "Total surrender is when you give up your right to yourself."

I wanted people to think I was "spiritual," and that was a hard battle. I had to take my spiritual reputation and hand it over to Christ. Surrender is the ultimate crisis because it is the ultimate battle. Picturing an image of who you are, and what you think other people think about you, your name, your work, and your spiritual reputation may help you determine where your battle is.

R E F L E C T I O N

Have you ever given your spiritual reputation over to Christ? In what ways have you lived in bondage to other people because you wanted them to think you are spiritual? Have you stepped beyond conversion toward surrender?

Prison Life

"Set me free from my prison, that I may praise Your name."   *(Psalm 142:7a)*

In his book *Born Again,* Charles Colson tells of his involvement in the Watergate scandal, his subsequent Christian conversion, and then his seven-month imprisonment. He describes what a struggle it was to keep a truly Christian spirit during his confinement.

He watched some of the strongest men finally give in and turn into ambulatory vegetables while in prison. Some slept every minute they could, as a way of escape. Some turned in on themselves and their very bodies followed their minds, brooding and drooping until they were bent over and shuffling around the prison. They degenerated both physically and mentally.

Colson says he avoided that only by the strongest determination—by strict physical disciplines like walking fast, exercising regularly, and fighting off sleep except at night, and by keeping his mind on God through regular Bible study and prayer. Only by a strict ordering of himself was he able to keep the prison from getting inside him.

Don't miss the simple but important lesson which God wants to teach us through this. Life never consists of just three dimensions: *time, space,* and *events.* There is always a *fourth—our response* to the three dimensions. Not *what* happens, and *where* and *when,* but *how we respond* to what happens. That's where the word *respon-*

sibility comes from: *our ability to respond.* A little poem I learned in school says it so succinctly:

> Two men looked out from prison bars.
> One saw mud, the other stars.

How easily we can become prisoners to self-pity and seething resentment. The darkness of our dungeon works to get inside of us and slowly but surely brings on the darkness of despair and depression. But, thank God, we have the *ability to respond* by turning to One who proclaims freedom for the captives!

R E F L E C T I O N
How often do you let the "dungeon get inside you"? In what ways have you learned to cope with the darkness of despair and depression?

The Subconscious Mind

"You were taught . . . to be made new in the attitude of your minds."   *(Ephesians 4:22a-23)*

Unconscious is a descriptive word attempting to portray the depths of your personality. The fact is that you never forget anything you experience. Though you may be not be able to recall it at will, anything that ever crossed your path lies in your memory. It is filed in the storeroom of your mind. This is both wonderful and terrible. It is both the misery and the grandeur of being a human.

Greatest of all, it means that if you let the Holy Spirit reach down deep, cleanse your subconscious mind and get into the depths of your heart to fill the storehouse of memory, God will give you power to actually make this one of the most creative parts of your personality.

Long ago I discovered the amazing power of the subconscious part of my mind in helping me prepare sermons. I have found that if weeks and months in advance, I feed certain basic ideas deep into my mind—a title, a brief outline, some thought of what I want to say—then the preacher doesn't simply work on the sermon. The sermon also works on the preacher!

One night in October 1920, in Toronto, Canada, Dr. Frederick G. Banting was working on his lecture for the following day. He was a young surgeon with such a small professional practice that he had to teach in order to make a living. For several hours Banting studied the literature on diabetes. It was scant for at that time medical science offered no means of control for the dreaded disease.

At a late hour he went wearily to bed, only to be suddenly awakened at two in the morning. His subconscious mind had some ideas to offer. He got up and wrote down three short sentences in his notebook, and then went back to sleep. Those three sentences led to the discovery of insulin. Banting's subconscious mind had come up with the solution when his conscious mind had found none. It was his subconscious mind which brought hope and life to millions of suffering people.

R E F L E C T I O N

What ideas do you need to feed into your mind so that they can work on you? Describe a time when you experienced the power of the subconscious mind.

Hold On to High Standards

"But among you there must not be even a hint of sexual immorality, or of any kind of impurity, or of greed, because these are improper for God's holy people."
(Ephesians 5:3)

Counselees have shared with me about their brothers and sisters, sometimes even parents, whose lives were filled with all kinds of immorality. But early in their childhood or youth, God used their very revulsion toward this to fill them with a determination to stay free from such sins and keep themselves pure for their marriage partners.

Do your dreams include high moral ideals for your courtship and marriage? Don't give up on those dreams. Hold on to them tenaciously. You who are not yet married, keep that vision before you. Don't sell those dreams for a mess of pottage by compromising your standards. Let me suggest an exercise that has helped others. Write an imaginary letter to your future bride or groom.

"But I don't know who that might be," you say. Never mind. Let me reword the suggestion. Write a *real* letter to your *imaginary* bride or groom. Make it a letter which you would like to give to the person on your wedding night, kind of a honeymoon note. Tell this person all about yourself and what you want to give him or her. Then tell what you are expecting on that wonderful night. It's a pretty sobering thought, isn't it? Terribly old-fashioned, awfully square? Yes, and highly Christian too.

REFLECTION

What kinds of things would you put in your honeymoon note? If married, what are some things that you would like to do to maintain purity in your marriage?

Who Goes There?

"For I have not come to call the righteous, but sinners."
(Matthew 9:13b)

The House of the Hapsburgs had ruled the Austro-Hungarian Empire since 1273 and the family had been a major political power in Europe until the Great War of 1914-1918. The funeral of Emperor Franz-Josef I of Austria was in November 1916. It was the last of the grandiose imperial funerals to be staged.

The Hapsburgs are buried in the family crypt located in the basement of the Capucin Monastery of Vienna. On the day of the funeral, the entire court assembled in full white dress, their hats covered with ostrich plumes. A military band played somber dirges and an anthem by Haydn. The cortege wound its way down stairs illumined with flaming torches, bearing the coffin draped in the imperial colors, black and gold. Finally it reached the great iron doors of the crypt, behind which stood the Cardinal-Archbishop of Vienna, along with his entourage of high church officials.

The officer in charge of the procession was the Court Marshal. As he approached the closed door and pounded on it with the hilt of his ceremonial sword, he followed a ceremony prescribed from time immemorial.

"Open!" he commanded.

"Who goes there?" intoned the Cardinal.

"We bear the remains of His Imperial and Apostolic

Majesty, Franz-Josef I, by the Grace of God Emperor of Austria, King of Hungary, Defender of the Faith, Prince of Bohemia-Moravia, Grand Duke of Lombardy, Venezia, Styrgia. . . ." And so on, through the *thirty-seven titles* of the Emperor.

"We know him not," replied the Cardinal, from beyond the door. "Who goes there?"

"We bear the remains of His Majesty, Franz-Josef I, Emperor of Austria and King of Hungary"—this very abbreviated form was allowed only in dire emergencies.

"We know him not," came the Cardinal's reply again. "Who goes there?"

"We bear the body of Franz-Josef, *our brother, a sinner like us all!*"

Whereupon, the massive doors swung slowly open and Franz-Josef was borne within.

> *For it is by grace you have been saved,*
> *through faith,*
> *and this not from yourselves,*
> *it is the gift of God.*

R E F L E C T I O N

How does it feel to know that grace is the only basis for entrance into the kingdom of God—on earth or in heaven? How could you help a non-Christian understand grace?

The Hound
of Heaven

---

*"Where can I go from Your Spirit? Where can I flee from
Your presence? If I go up to the heavens, you are there; if
I make my bed in the depths, you are there."*
                                    (Psalm 139:7-8)

While I was preaching at a university, a student
named Jack came to counsel with me. Like
many other preachers' kids, he was rebelling
against the faith of his parents and his own preteen conversion experience. He told me his story with deep
shame.

In his attempt to run from God, he had deliberately
dated a girl well known on campus for her loose morals.
They had faked a signout to go to their homes for the
weekend but ended up spending the night together in a
motel. However, what he had fantasized as a night of
ecstatic pleasure turned out to be quite different. Now he
felt guilty, empty and, worst of all, abandoned by God. He
kept saying to me, "I just can't seem to find Him again."

I kept answering, "What you really mean, Jack, is you
can't get away from Him."

He asked me to explain what I had said, for it was
the opposite of what he felt. I opened my Bible to Psalm
139:7-8, handed it to him, and asked him to read it aloud.

Then I asked, "Jack, who do you think you met in
that motel room?"

He looked puzzled. "I don't understand. Do you mean
the...the girl?"

I replied, "No, no, Jack. I mean God. Don't you realize when you tried to run from God, you ran right smack into Him that night in the motel? In fact, God was never nearer than then."

Big tears began to trickle down his cheeks. Soon we were praying to the One who had never stopped seeking His wayward son. God's love had never changed, only His strategy. Jack learned you can refuse God's love, but you can't lose it when the Hound of Heaven is on your trail!

Sometimes God seeks us by letting us go our own way and allowing us to suffer the inevitable consequences of that way in the hope that our suffering will bring us back to Him.

R E F L E C T I O N

What are some times when God has let you go your own way? What were the consequences? How do you feel knowing that "God was never nearer" to you than then?

The Value
of Anger

*"In your anger do not sin; when you are on your beds,
search your hearts and be silent."*
                                        (Psalm 4:4)

Did you ever stop to consider how much good has
been accomplished in the world when good people finally got angry enough at wrong to do
something about it?

Martin Luther said, "When I am angry, I preach well
and pray better." Dr. William Channing said, "Ordinarily,
I weigh 120 pounds, but when I'm mad I weigh a ton!"
The history of reform is replete with illustrations.

English prisoners used to be kept in vile, disease-
ridden prisons that were described as a veritable hell-on-
earth. But John Howard and his followers got angry and
did something about it.

Slavery was a deeply entrenched evil in this New
World until men like William Lloyd Garrison "saw in the
sorrowful face of the slave the shadowed face of God."
Nerved by a righteous anger that would not be silenced,
Garrison shouted, "I will not retreat a single inch. And I
will be heard!"

Young Abe Lincoln, watching a slave market for the
first time, got sick to his stomach and a passionate white-
hot anger arose in him. His fingernails bit into his hands
and he whispered so fiercely that everyone heard him,
"That's wrong, and if I ever get a chance to hit it, I'll hit it
hard!"

Military hospitals were horrible until Florence Nightingale came along. One of her biographers presents her not as a gentle angel of mercy, but as a stubborn, angry woman with a clear call from God to unrelentingly pursue government officials until they provided humane treatment for the wounded and the dying. Those officials shuddered at the mention of her name.

Anger is not necessarily the opposite of love. Sometimes it is the result of love and its clearest expression. Never pray for your anger to be removed or taken away from you. That's as mistaken and immature as asking God to remove all sexual desires from your life. Pray rather that your temper be cleansed and brought under the Spirit's control. Pray not that anger be *eradicated,* but that it be *redirected* to that which makes God angry.

R E F L E C T I O N

Did you ever stop to consider that maybe the reason your love for Christ is so lukewarm, or even cold, is because you do not get angry enough, do not hate evil enough? In what ways does your anger need to be redirected?

D e b t - C o l l e c t i n g

"Forgive us our debts, as we forgive our debtors."
                                    (Matthew 6:12, KJV)

In the Parable of the Unmerciful Servant, Jesus put into living color and stereophonic sound His teachings about forgiveness. This parable is filled with profound insights about spiritual and emotional healing.

A king decided to settle his accounts and found that one servant owed him the fantastic sum of 10 million dollars. A servant working for a few cents a day could never save up enough money to repay this debt, but in his pride, he fell on his knees, begging for patience and an extension of time.

The king in his mercy gave the servant far more than he asked for; he released him and forgave him all his debts.

But the servant couldn't receive, live, or enjoy his freedom. Because he didn't understand that his debt had been canceled, a vicious circle began. He thought he still owed, so he thought he still had to pay and collect debts from others. When he came across a fellow worker who owed him a measly twenty bucks, he seized him by the throat and said, "Pay me what you owe me." When the coworker couldn't do it, he was sent to jail.

The unforgiven and unforgiving person is plagued with guilt and resentment. Like the servant, he eventually finds himself living in a prison house where he is tortured by all manner of inner emotional conflicts, and broken relationships are the result.

Think of how you apply this to the significant others in your life: the *parents* who hurt you when you were growing up; *brothers* and *sisters* who failed you, teased you, and put you down when you needed help; a *friend* who betrayed you; a *sweetheart* who rejected you; your *marriage partner* who promised to love, honor, comfort, and care for you but instead has nagged, scapegoated, or caused you pain.

The good news is that there is a way to deal with all these hurts from the past. God's way goes far beyond forgiving and surrendering resentment. God takes sins, failures, and hurts that happened earlier in our lives and wraps His loving purposes around them to change them. Because He has set us free, we can set others free and thereby set in motion grace and love.

R E F L E C T I O N

Are guilt and resentment keeping you emotionally imprisoned today? Is there someone you resent, someone you've never let off the hook?

A Childhood Motto

"Therefore, there is now no condemnation for those who are in Christ Jesus."   *(Romans 8:1)*

A few years ago I attended a Holy Spirit conference in Michigan. One day a pastor named Brad shared with us that for many years he had been a struggling, up-and-down Christian. Outwardly he was a very successful pastor with a record of considerable acomplishment. But inwardly he was like a yo-yo, bouncing between spiritual highs and lows. Or like a billiard ball batting from one side to another, hitting pride on one side and condemnation, guilt, and depression on the other.

Brad told us his story.

"A couple of years ago, there came to me a flash of insight from the Holy Spirit. I suddenly realized that my life was not really being ruled by love for God and for other people. Instead, for the past forty-nine years a little childhood motto instilled in me by my parents had really been running my life. All those years I thought Christ controlled my life, until I became aware that it was a motto I had adopted in my early years."

What was the powerful childhood motto? "Measure up!" Brad continued.

"I'm sure my parents didn't mean to give me this impression, but what I heard them saying was, 'Sure, we love you, but we would love you more if only you would measure up!' "

The Holy Spirit began to help Brad look at himself and see the real motivation of his life. He realized that those two simple words, carried over from his childhood, were affecting him in all his present relationships, including his relationship with God. For forty-nine years he had never felt he could measure up.

"But now at last I am gaining freedom from that childhood motto and am learning true freedom in the Holy Spirit."

R E F L E C T I O N

Does a childhood motto rule your life? Does the Holy Spirit control and direct your life? Or is it an immature, childish spirit from your past? Or maybe it is a combination?

We're Not Worthy

*"For great is Your love toward me; You have delivered
me from the depths of the grave."*
                                        (Psalm 86:13)

In the second century, a critic of Christianity named
Celsus said the idea of God loving *sinners—bad
people*—was "a thing unheard of in any other religion." He was absolutely right. That's what grace is about.
That's what makes it different from other religions; they
offer *good views* and *good advice*—"Be good, straighten
up your life, clean up your act, get it together, live a good
life and then, of course, you can come to God. Then you
will be pleasing to God and He will love you." Only the
Gospel of Christ is good news, the incredible message of
grace. As A.W. Tozer put it, "Grace is the good pleasure
of God that inclines Him to bestow benefit upon the
undeserving."

During the Napoleanic Wars, a young, battle-weary
French soldier fell asleep while on guard duty. He was
court-martialed, found guilty, and sentenced to death.
His widowed mother somehow arranged an audience
with the Emperor Napoleon himself. Falling prostrate at
his feet she begged for her son's life to be spared, explain-
ing he was her only child and her sole means of support.
Napoleon grew weary of her pleas.

"Madam, your son does not deserve mercy. He
deserves to die," he said coldly. To which the mother
immediately replied, "Of course, Sire, you are right.

That's why I am asking you to show mercy on him. If he were deserving, it wouldn't be mercy." Napoleon was so touched by the logic of her statement that he pardoned the soldier.

If we were deserving, it wouldn't be grace. It is undeserved and unmerited. It is God's free gift, completely unobstructed by our sin, our guilt, and our unworthiness.

REFLECTION

Do you think that God expects you to live up to certain standards of performance? Why or why not? Have you ever felt that the continuation of God's gift of grace depends on how well you perform? Why or why not?

The Ultimate Will

"And we know that in all things God works for the good of those who love Him, who have been called according to His purpose."   *(Romans 8:28)*

ible scholar William Barclay of Glasgow University was a prolific writer. Barclay's famous commentaries on the New Testament are known around the world and have been translated into many languages. While many would not agree with some of his theological conclusions, Barclay's commentaries are unexcelled for background material on the New Testament. "How did William Barclay do it?" is a question that has been asked over and over again. Writing newspaper columns, authoring books, appearing on TV programs, working as a dean of a college, taking time to be with students and to listen to them—how did he do it? In a manner different than most of us will ever employ.

You see, some years ago when William Barclay discovered that he was going deaf, he was faced with a decision: *Should he turn in on himself in self-pity and end his career?* What a blow! Would anyone say that deafness was God's intended, perfect will for William Barclay or for anyone else? I doubt it. But knowing himself to be within the circle of God's permissive, circumstantial will, and grasping all the power in the promise of Romans 8:28, William Barclay decided that he would make use of his new world of almost total silence. Shut off from all

the other sounds of life, he gave himself in total concentration to the inner sounds of God's Word. Even when a
hearing aid did help, he would often shut it off in order to
be in a world of silence. Instead of self-pity, he wrapped
Romans 8:28 around his deafness and used it to work out
God's purpose through his life.

R E F L E C T I O N
What kinds of struggles have you had with understanding
God's will for your life? How does the promise found in
Romans 8:28 make you feel about God's purpose for your
life?

Choose Your Pain

---

*"No discipline seems pleasant at the time, but painful.
Later on, however, it produces a harvest of righteous-
ness and peace for those who have been trained by it."*
(Hebrews 12:11)

J im and Claire sat together on a couch before me at
their first counseling session. Claire was obviously
embarrassed and reached for a Kleenex before we
got started. Jim started by telling me all the good things
about their marriage.

Finally the discord was sounded—Claire's seemingly
uncontrollable temper which, like a sudden storm, could
strike out of nowhere and leave a path of destruction in
its wake. And when I say "strike," that was what Claire
literally did both verbally and physically.

It happened the first time a few days after the honeymoon. It was a terrible shock to both of them, and they
cried and prayed together about it. But the incidents
continued. Now they were expecting a child and were
both scared of what might happen.

During their lengthy courtship, Claire had shared her
family's problem of verbal and physical abuse with Jim,
but told him she hated it so much she was sure she could
never be like that!

This is perhaps the most deceptive thing about such
problems. We think that because we grew up hating these
family characteristics and telling ourselves, "We will
never be like that!" we are rid of them. And so we deny

them, and often they go deeper into our personalities. Unknown to us, they become a part of our own actions and reactions. And someday when we try to form intimate relationships, they explode with the force of a volcano.

"You need to choose your pain," I told Jim and Claire. "In some ways, it could be easier for you to limp along as you have been, choosing to bear your present pain. At least you know it and in that sense are comfortable with it. Or, you can choose a different kind of pain—the pain of confronting the truth about yourself and your family. You're in pain now; for a time you'll be in pain again, but it will be a productive pain that leads to wholeness."

By the grace of God they chose the right pain, so that healing and joy and harmonious love increasingly became the pattern of their marriage. No—not perfect, but good enough to maintain stability even when their child was in the throes of "the terrible twos."

R E F L E C T I O N

Do you need to choose a different pain from what you are now experiencing? How would it feel to confront the truth about yourself or your family?

The Great Alchemist

"I will turn the darkness into light before them and make the rough places smooth. These are the things I will do; I will not forsake them."

(Isaiah 42:16b)

Too often we quote Romans 8:28 out of context: "And we know that God causes all things to work together for good to those who love God" (NASB). The *King James Version* of this verse can be misleading: "All things work together for good. . . ." Unfortunately the *things* do not; they may even work against us. But *God* works in and through the things, causing circumstances to work out for our good. That's different, for it turns the emphasis from fate to a Father, a Person of love and design. That God causes all things to work together for good is the greatest part of the entire healing process; that He can change hurtful insights to helpful outreach is the greatest miracle of all.

Total healing is more than soothing painful memories, more than forgiving and begin forgiven of harmful resentments, even more than the reprogramming of our minds. Healing is the miracle of God's recycling grace, where He actually recycles our hang-ups into wholeness and usefulness.

This doesn't mean that God is the *Author* of all events, but He is the *Master* of all events. Nothing has ever happened to you that God cannot use for good if you will surrender it into His hands and allow Him to work.

God does not change the actual, factual nature of the evil which occurs. But God can change the *meaning* of it for your total life. God is the great Alchemist who can take every damage, every hurt, every crippling infirmity, and turn it all into spiritual gold.

When you cooperate with the Holy Spirit in this process of deep prayer and inner healing, God will reweave the design of your life and recycle it into a means of serving others. Then you will be able to look at it and say with the psalmist, "The Lord has done this, and it is marvelous in [my] eyes" (Psalm 118:23).

R E F L E C T I O N

How might God be using the emotional damage, hurts, and crippling weaknesses of your life to create a beautiful new design? What would you like to see God do through you in the lives of other people as the result of His healing work in your life?

THE SURE ROAD TO

MATURITY IS TO

LEARN TO LIVE

ABOVE MOODS AND

FEELINGS.

The Sin Shredder

"When you were dead in your sins . . . God made you alive with Christ."   *(Colossians 2:13)*

Dottie was a single young adult who came for counsel. She wasn't the least bit hesitant about sharing herself openly. I was struck by what seemed to be an almost compulsive need to reveal the garbage of her life in lurid detail.

Dottie would pause occasionally in her x-rated recital and say with a confident smile, "Now I don't want you to get any idea that I feel guilty about this."

I must admit to a perversity which leads me to play the game with this type, and so I would say, "Oh no, of course not. I understand—no guilt."

Then I began to observe some body language from Dottie, as she kept taking sheets of Kleenex from the box I keep on a side table. Not to wipe away tears—naturally not—since she felt no guilt; but one by one, shredding the tissues into little pieces. The pile on the table grew higher and higher. What fascinated me most was that she was completely unaware of the shredding ritual.

After a while, I said rather abruptly, "Excuse me, Dottie, but I don't believe your story about not feeling guilty about all this garbage in your life. In fact, I have the feeling your pile of guilt is as high as the mountain of Kleenex you've made on the table there."

She looked down in shocked disbelief. Obviously embarrassed, she sat silently staring at the shredded tissues. I was silent, but the Holy Spirit spoke loud and clear. Slowly Dottie reached for another Kleenex, and this time made proper use of it.

"You're right," she sniffled. "I think I was hoping I'd not feel guilty if I was just honest about my sins. But down deep I knew better, and I guess I was really hoping you wouldn't let me get by with it."

We read together Colossians 2:13-15 where Paul describes Christ's work on the cross. Dottie came to understand that she didn't need to tear up either her sins or her Kleenex. Christ had shredded all her sins on the cross and set her free from their guilt, if she would but confess them to Him and trust what He had done for her.

R E F L E C T I O N

Have you ever tried to ignore or deny guilt about something? In what interesting ways did your guilt reveal itself?

Unconditional Surrender

"The weapons we fight with are not the weapons of the world. On the contrary, they have divine power to demolish strongholds. We demolish arguments and every pretension that sets itself up against the knowledge of God, and we take captive every thought to make it obedient to Christ."   *(2 Corinthians 10:4-5)*

One of the most exciting and interesting experiences of our missionary career was to witness the transfer of power from Britain to India. We gathered with thousands on August 15, 1947 to watch as the British flag (the Union Jack) was slowly lowered and the tricolor flag of the newly independent India was hoisted in its place. The local police band added a touch of humor by playing "London Bridge Is Falling Down!" In spite of the musical selection, it was an awesome and exciting hour.

But I have had an even greater privilege—of being with hundreds of people when, through the wisdom and the power of God, ancient strongholds of childishness, infirmity, and immaturity were pulled down and the Christian flag raised up.

But before this could happen there was always a series of struggles. These took many forms which involved all parts of the total personality—mind, emotion, and will. There were many major and minor skirmishes, in which childish things were done away with. Ultimately there came the decisive battle when the full surrender was made, when the defeated and oftentimes battered self ran up the white flag of unconditional surrender. Then the Christian flag was hoisted and Christ could claim full lordship over His own.

Have you ever noticed what the Christian flag really is? It is simply a clean white flag with the cross imprinted on a small section of blue. It is the emblem of the conquering Christ implanted on the sign of our surrender.

R E F L E C T I O N

What strongholds of childishness, infirmity, or immaturity need to be broken down in your life? Will the skirmishes be major or minor? Why?

Know the Difference

"When you are tempted, He will also provide a way out so that you can stand up under it."

(1 Corinthians 10:13b)

Temptation is *not* sin. A thought of evil is not sin, but allowing it to settle down until it becomes evil thinking is sin. Having the desire is not sin; accepting the evil suggestion to fulfill that desire in the wrong way is sin.

Brent, a college youth, came to counsel with me. After listening to his camouflage of so-called intellectual difficulties he was having with the Christian faith, I asked, "Why don't you tell me what's really bothering you?" He did. He was angry with God. "Why?" I asked. "What did He do to you?" He replied, "That's the problem; it's what He *didn't* do for me. Last year during the Spiritual Emphasis Week I asked Him to take away my sexual desires. The struggle was too much, so I asked Him to remove them."

Brent's real problem was he had never gotten clear in his mind the distinction between temptation and sin. We spent a long time together until he saw it clearly. When he was able to see the foolishness of his anger against God, he could be restored in his Christian walk. Years later I had the privilege of performing his marriage ceremony to an attractive Christian young lady. At the reception he whispered to me, "I'm sure glad God didn't answer that prayer." I laughingly replied, "Amen!"

Don't ask God to take away your sexual desires or your ambitions, or to remove your temper from you. He cannot answer these prayers. He can and will give you self-control over your sexual desires. He can enable you to have one all-consuming ambition—His glory. And He can cleanse and redirect your temper so that, like Jesus, you will get angry at the things you ought to get angry at. Know the difference between temptation and sin.

R E F L E C T I O N

Have you ever asked God to remove sexual desires, ambitions, or anger from your life? How did He respond? In what ways has God provided you with self-control in these areas?

Divine Expectations

"Therefore no one will be declared righteous in His sight by observing the law; rather, through the law we become conscious of sin."

(Romans 3:20)

I am often amazed at the incredible assumptions some performance-minded and perfectionistic Christians live with. I listened to Angela tell me all the things for which she felt guilty. Her list got longer and longer, and she became very emotional as she heaped failure after failure on herself. Lines of strain showed on her face. It was obvious she was, as she put it, "living on the nub."

The more we talked, the deeper she dug herself into a quagmire of depression. I had to do something to break the melancholy spell. I leaned forward and said eagerly, "Angela, may I touch you?"

She looked startled and backed away from me. "What?"

Again I asked her, "May I touch you? You see, it's been a long time since I've seen such a divine being."

"What do you mean?"

"What I mean, Angela, is that only some kind of god-like creature could expect to do all the things you listed, let alone do them perfectly. You have absolutely divine expectations. Where did you ever get the notion that you or anyone else were expected to do all those things? What I hear you saying is you feel guilty because you can't do everything and do it flawlessly."

Angela sat silently for quite a while. Then she hung her head and cried quietly.

"Do you know what I'm thinking?" she asked. "It's crazy and I'm ashamed to tell you. But this confirms what has been dawning on me lately. Somewhere a long time ago, I began to take seriously what my folks used to call me, 'Angel.' I can't believe it. I felt they expected so much of me that I began to play the part of an angel. I can't put all the blame on them—I brought a lot of this on myself, trying to feel special."

It was a Spirit-revealed moment of self-awareness which started Angela on a new pilgrimage of grace and freedom from the performance trap.

R E F L E C T I O N

What kinds of "divine expectations" have you had for yourself? For others?

Life's Great Interrupters

"My grace is sufficient for you, for My power is made perfect in weakness." (2 Corinthians 12:9a)

One of life's great interrupters is *an unplanned pregnancy.* Many a distraught wife has come for help and said through bitter tears:
"I don't understand how this could have happened. We were doing everything we could to prevent it. But mainly I can't understand why God allowed it. It's the worst thing that could have happened to us at this time. Our other children are just getting to the age where I could be free to...."

Then she shares her plans for finishing a long-awaited degree, or getting a job which would finally enable them to live without financial worries, or joining with her husband in more direct Christian service. Don't underestimate the emotional and spiritual struggle that this unchosen dungeon of delay can bring to even the finest women. However, this is where we see a great divide between the pro-abortion and pro-life people.

The pro-abortion advocates don't understand God's promise of "sufficient grace." With Christians, while there are many unplanned pregnancies, there are few unwanted children. Years later, those very same wives joyfully share their pride and joy in these children, and then go on to tell the wonderful way God used those years to bring them to a new depth of intimacy with Himself.

Interrupted dreams are not necessarily broken dreams meant to be abandoned. They are only delayed dreams meant to be postponed. Remember, God-given dreams will keep in the deep-freeze of acceptance, provided you keep out any heat from resentments. Then, at a later time, you can thaw them in the microwave of freshly warmed hope and determination.

R E F L E C T I O N

What kinds of interruptions to your life plan have you experienced? Did you find that your dreams were merely postponed? Why or why not?

Letting In
the Light

"For light is capable of showing up everything for what it really is." (Ephesians 5:13-14, PH)

L ight and truth have a close connection. Light enables us to see the truth, respond to it, and then experience new life.

Several experiences in India made me appreciate Paul's definition of light in Ephesians 5. Every year we attended a large Christian convention in the middle of a forest. After everyone had retired to their tents and put out their lanterns, the forest was pitch dark. One night a woman awakened, suffering from a bad headache. Not wanting to disturb her friends, she quietly began feeling around in the tent-pocket nearest her cot until she found the tube of mentholated salve she had brought. She vigorously rubbed it all over her forehead until its cooling, analgesic properties relieved her headache and she was able to go back to sleep. Imagine her chagrin, and her companions' hilarity, when the morning light revealed that she had smeared a mint-flavored toothpaste all over her forehead!

Another incident at the same encampment wasn't quite as funny. My mother and dad had retired for the night, safely tucked in under their mosquito nets. Mother, a light sleeper, heard a strange sound in the tent. Dad was asleep and protested when she woke him up.

"Go back to sleep; it's probably some stray dog looking for scraps left from supper."

But Mom insisted until Dad reluctantly shined his big flashlight into the darkness. No, it wasn't a dog; it was a ten-foot python crawling between their cots! You can be sure Dad was wide awake by the time he killed it. Again, it was light that made things visible and revealed the snake for what it really was.

John reminds us, "God is light; in Him there is no darkness at all." So, to "walk in the light, as He is in the light" (1 John 1:5, 7) means to make a conscious decision to not keep any area of life "in the dark." Rather, we choose to open ourselves fully to God's light; and if we see something we thought was a harmless dog but turns out to be a dangerous snake, we will ask God to get rid of it.

REFLECTION

What areas of your life have you kept "in the dark"? How do you feel about God's light making darkened areas of your life visible?

The Root
of the Problem

"See to it that no one misses the grace of God and that no bitter root grows up to cause trouble and defile many."   *(Hebrews 12:15)*

For both Gladys and her husband it was a second marriage. Their experiences were remarkably similar—their spouses had simply taken off with someone else and left the children with them. They had both lived as single parents for several years, had met in church, married, and now felt God had given them a wonderful second chance for a Christian family. Their children got along remarkably well. There was only one major problem.

Gladys couldn't understand why her stepson, Mike, always seemed to rub her the wrong way. He was not a problem child and was affectionate and obedient to her. But Gladys had a strange sense of hostility toward him that resulted in her being harsh and overdemanding. Naturally it was beginning to affect the marriage and the whole family. We counseled together and prayed about it several times, but the mystery remained.

One day we talked about how her first husband, Ted, an alcoholic, had badly mistreated her. In the middle of the conversation she became silent. Sensing that the Great Counselor had taken over, I too kept quiet and inwardly prayed. After some time she began to express herself slowly, with long pauses in between.

"I think I know what my problem is...I never

realized it before. . .I see a great many of Ted's characteristics in Mike. . .my goodness, he even looks something
like him. . .has the same kind of build. . .and
mannerisms. . .I can't believe it. . .he reminds me of him
and that triggers off a lot of deeply buried hurts in
me. . .and I've just realized, I don't think I've fully forgiv-
en Ted for what he did to me."

Gladys began to cry softly, "You know, I've been taking out my feelings on Mike and he's completely inno-
cent."

Now we knew what we should be praying about. It
was a beautiful sight to see the forgiving, healing grace of
the Cross cleanse away both the past source and the present stimulation for her anger. It was only a matter of
time until they were enjoying a new level of loving relationships in the family.

R E F L E C T I O N
Take a recent situation where you got angry and ask
yourself these questions: What was I really so angry
about? Against whom was I actually angry? Why did this
(person/situation) make me so angry?

The Trap of
Self-Contempt

"Love your neighbor as yourself."
(Matthew 22:39b)

St. Augustine said many wonderful things, but he also made some horrendous blunders. It has taken us centuries to get over some of his extremities regarding the body and sex and self. One of those blunders is in *The City of God:* "The difference between the city of the world and the city of God is that the one is characterized by love of self to the contempt of God, and the other (the city of God) is characterized by love of God to the contempt of self." This is very wrong, very unbiblical, and the way many of us live. We think we are pleasing God, that we are producing a sanctified and holy life through this kind of counterfeit holiness. In reality, we produce a guilt-ridden piety, a joyless self-negation, an unattractive goodness. Instead of delivering us from self-centeredness and pride, self-contempt leads us into a religious self-centeredness and pride.

In C.S. Lewis' famous *Screwtape Letters,* that abominable demon Screwtape gives some subtle advice to his assistant Wormwood on this matter. Referring to the young Christian he is tempting as the patient, Screwtape writes to Wormwood, "You must therefore conceal from the patient the true end of humility. Let him think of it not as self-forgetfulness but as a certain kind of opinion (namely, a low opinion) of his own talents and character."

Self-despising is not pleasing to God, and it is not the

answer to the problem of pride. It actually increases the problem. Psychologist Karen Horney has said, "Self-hate is pride's inseparable companion, and you can't have one without the other." How often self-incrimination becomes an inverted form of good works, of inner penance which we must do, thinking we are pleasing to God. Then an amazing thing happens: condemnation of self becomes the basis of "a good conscience."

The heart of the Christian life is love, loving God with the whole self and loving others as you love yourself. This requires not less of a self, but more of a self filled with power and love.

R E F L E C T I O N

What are some times when others have used selflessness as spiritual or emotional blackmail on you? Have there been times when selflessness has been the goal of your Christian life?

The Grand Chasm

"For all have sinned and fall short of the glory of God, and are justified freely by His grace through the redemption that came by Christ Jesus."
                                    (Romans 3:23-24)

I 'll never forget the first time I saw the Grand Canyon of Arizona. I was an MK (missionary's kid) who had seen many of the so-called wonders of the world. I had learned the hard way that the reality of sightseeing rarely lived up to the fantasy surrounding its advertising. So by the age of twelve I had already developed the practical philosophy of, "Don't get too excited about a famous sight, because it's not going to live up to your expectations."

It was in that skeptical spirit I approached the Grand Canyon in 1934. In those relatively uncommercialized days, you simply walked toward it and suddenly, there it was before you. I was shocked speechless and stood for a long time in sheer disbelief at the utter vastness of its size—the width, the breadth, the height of the chasm with that tiny ribbon of a river at the bottom—and the incredible spectrum of changing colors. It took several minutes to actually take it all in, to realize it was true. For the first time in my life the experience of something actually surpassed my expectations!

That's the picture which comes to my mind when I think of another chasm, greater even than the Grand Canyon—the chasm which exists between a perfect, holy

God and imperfect, sinful human beings. It is a moral Grand Canyon and even more vast and unbridgeable. How can we get across this abyss? How can we bridge the gap?

The truth is that we cannot, and this leaves us in an impossible predicament. God's Word makes it plain there is no way to negotiate a reconciliation from our side of the chasm. If it's ever to be bridged, it must be done from God's side. There is nothing we humans can do to meet the requirements of God's perfect law. Make no mistake about it—those requirements have not changed. His purpose for us is the same. He made us to live in perfect relationship with Himself and others, and He still wills our complete perfection.

R E F L E C T I O N

In what ways have you attempted to meet the requirements of God's law? Were you successful? Why or why not?

Courage to
Face the Pain

"Love your enemies, do good to those who hate you,
bless those who curse you, pray for those who mistreat
you."   *(Luke 6:27-28)*

In spite of her dedication to Christ and a consistent devotional life, Margaret's marriage and family were being affected by her outbursts of anger and serious bouts with depression. It didn't take long to discover that she had internalized the voice of an unpleasant, perfectionistic mother until she thought it was the voice of conscience and God. Now she was her own harshest taskmaster, demanding perfection of herself, even as others had demanded it of her. Hurt, anger, and guilt kept the treadmill going. Margaret needed to face the hurts and then forgive those who had hurt her.

During one of our prayer times for the healing of some painful memories, a scene emerged which she had not shared with me. She said she had not wanted to look at it, but while we were praying, God gave her the courage to face the pain. She was just a youngster practicing for her first piano recital. She wanted to play her piece perfectly, and so she worked and worked, until the piece was memorized.

At the recital, she played it perfectly. As she walked off the stage, her piano teacher grasped her elbow and said softly, "Excellent, Margaret, you played it perfectly!" She was so excited. But when she took her place beside her mother, there was a pause and then this whisper in her ear, "Your slip was showing the whole time."

Margaret sobbed as she told God about this, and about many other scars. Best of all, she received grace to forgive, and also to be forgiven for the resentments she had carried for years. It was the crisis beginning to a process of change—from living under the law to living under grace.

R E F L E C T I O N

Do you have resentments that you have been carrying for years? Are there hurts that you need to face and/or people you need to forgive who have caused those hurts? What or who are they?

The Impossibilities
of God

"*Every good and perfect gift is from above, coming down from the Father of the heavenly lights, who does not change like shifting shadows.*"

(James 1:17)

Can God do anything? With God all things are possible, aren't they? We must all come to understand the flip side to the verse we hear so often, namely, that with God some things are *impossible*. God's power is unlimited except by His own moral nature and by certain self-imposed limitations He has built into His world, including the moral beings He has created. So the best place to begin getting this whole matter straight is to think about some of the things God cannot and will not do.

First, God cannot violate His nature. God's power is unlimited, but it is morally conditioned—it is limited by His perfect nature of holy love. He cannot cease from being God for a while. He cannot act out of character. Thus God cannot lie or sin or commit any moral evil. Of course, this also means that from a moral standpoint God cannot change.

Second, God cannot violate His own laws. This is the only world that we as humans have to live in and we are the only moral creatures of our kind. By creating this kind of a world, God has imposed certain limitations on Himself.

Let me use an extreme illustration. Let's say that

through some tragic accident your leg is amputated above the knee. Would you pray that God would grow a new leg for you? Why not? You would correctly reply that God just doesn't do things that way. Certainly in the final resurrection that leg will be fully restored, but not in this life.

Finally, God cannot violate human freedom. He has created a race of persons with freedom to make choices. Let's think of how God works regarding our salvation. God desires to save us from our sins, make us His redeemed children, and change us so we will love and serve Him—and do all this without at any point overriding our freedom. That would destroy what He most desires—our freely chosen love.

God can do anything except not be God!

REFLECTION

Why is it important to have a God who can't do some things? How does a better understanding of God's self-imposed limitations affect your prayer life and expectations of God?

Hidden Anger

"[Love] is not easily angered, it keeps no record of wrongs."   *(1 Corinthians 13:5b)*

Many years ago, a professor at a Christian college called me and said, "I remember you saying, 'Whenever you experience a response on your part that is way out of proportion to the stimulus, then look out. You have probably tapped into some deeply hidden emotional hurt.' I guess that it has happened to me."

So he came to our town, and we spent almost a week together. He was a learned, highly spiritual man, but there had been a confrontation on that college campus, and all of a sudden this controlled, Christian scholar was reacting in violent anger. *Rage* was really the word for it. He was shocked at himself, and felt so guilty. No amount of Scripture reading or praying or trying to leave the whole situation with God seemed to help. In agony he confessed to me: "I actually felt as if I wanted to kill somebody."

It wasn't hard to find the roots of the problem, but he had trouble accepting them. He kept saying, "Oh, but that's so silly...it can't be that!" But I encouraged him to tell me anyway.

He had been a bright, precocious child, an egghead almost from birth. He was always first in the classroom but last on the playground. Every recess was a hell for him. Rougher and tougher children had teased, made fun of, bullied, tortured, knocked down, and physically hurt this intelligent but uncoordinated little boy. More than that, they made an emotional cripple out of him. He was amazed at the sensitivity of his memory. He remembered all the children by name, and even what they wore. It was all there, though years had elapsed, and he tapped into this fountain of rage. As we went through every incident, he called each youngster by name. We put everyone under his forgiveness.

"Will you forgive Dan? Will you forgive Sally? And will you forgive...?"

Does this sound trivial? Quite the contrary, it was incredibly painful. But in prayer he found grace to forgive each one of those kids who had made life so intolerable for him. The Holy Spirit took the sting out of those memories and defused their compulsive power. That was the beginning of an in-depth change.

R E F L E C T I O N

How did you deal with your anger as a child? Do you find yourself unusually sensitive to certain "unjust situations"?

A Designer Creation

"Love the Lord your God with all your heart and with all your soul and with all your mind....Love your neighbor as yourself." (Matthew 22:37, 39b)

Many Christians have adopted the idea that true Christian humility really means self-belittling. The truth is that self-belittling runs counter to some very basic teachings of the Christian faith. The great commandment is that we love God with all our being. The second commandment is an extension of the first—that we love our neighbor as we love our-selves. Actually, we have three commandments here: to love God, to love yourself, and to love others. The term *self-love* has a wrong connotation for some people. Whether you call it self-esteem or self-worth, it is plainly the foundation of Christian love for others. And this is the opposite of what many Christians believe.

Years ago, after I preached a sermon about these two great commandments of Jesus, a man said to me, "As old as I am, I have never before actually heard Jesus' Word correctly. I suddenly realized that with my lips I have said, 'Love thy neighbor as thyself,' but deep down in my inner self I have really been hearing, 'Love thy neighbor but hate thyself.' I'm afraid I have been scrupulously living up to the commandment as I translated it."

Do you need to get your theology straightened out? Have you said to yourself, "Well, I know God loves me, but I just can't stand myself." This is the expression of subtly hidden resentment against your Creator. When you despise His creation, you are really saying that you don't like the design or care much for the Designer. You are failing to realize how much God loves you and how much you mean to Him.

From where will you get your idea of yourself? From false ideas and wrong theology? Or will you say, "I am going to listen to God's opinion of me, and let Him reprogram me until His estimate of me becomes a part of my life, right down to my innermost feelings"?

R E F L E C T I O N
What connotation does the term "self-love" hold for you? Do you have a tendency to either overestimate or underestimate your own value and abilities? How can you become a partner with God in renewing the way you think about yourself?

Facing the Truth

"You intended to harm me, but God intended it for good."   *(Genesis 50:20a)*

For the first time in her life, Dolores got up nerve enough to tell about being sexually abused by her father. It began when she was six and continued until she was nine. Finally she could bear it no longer and told her mother about it. Her mother became furious, gave her a severe beating, and accused her of deliberately "seducing" her father.

With painful tears, Dolores shared her story with the evangelist visiting the church I was pastoring. She then asked what she could do to be free from her seemingly unresolvable feelings of guilt. He told her she would never get rid of those feelings "until she repented before God of her own responsibility in the matter." She was utterly shattered by his advice and came near to breaking under the newly added load of guilt.

It's a tribute to her sheer desperation and the grace of God that Dolores ever came to see me—another preacher. And I must confess I was so angry at that evangelist I could hardly control myself. Can you understand the layers of guilt Dolores had to work through? Her mother accusing her of seduction; the evangelist representing the voice of God and reinforcing her mother's judgment of her.

Again and again, I pointed out to her how ridiculous it was to blame a six-year-old child for seducing a grown man. But she simply could not admit how wrong both her mother and dad had been and how deeply they had hurt her. Dolores was the perfect example of so many damaged Christians. They would rather take all the blame for what someone did to them than face the truth about the persons who did it.

As long as we are untruthful in our hearts, the Holy Spirit cannot free us from our feelings of guilt and give us lasting peace. Dolores needed help in acknowledging how badly she had been hurt by the betrayal of her parents. Then she needed to forgive them, and ask God to forgive her for resenting them. It was the beginning of a new life of inner peace for Dolores.

R E F L E C T I O N
In what situations have you found yourself willing to take the blame for what someone did to you rather than face the painful truth? Are you having trouble sorting out your responsibility and actual guilt?

WE CAN REFUSE THE

LOVE OF GOD, BUT

WE CANNOT STOP HIM

FROM LOVING US.

A Modern Samson

"The Spirit of the Lord is on Me, because He has anointed Me to preach good news to the poor. He has sent Me to proclaim freedom for the prisoners and recovery of sight for the blind, to release the oppressed, to proclaim the year of the Lord's favor."

(Luke 4:18-19)

Claire is a homemaker who in desperation attempted to end her life. However, like many others, she admitted that she had hoped she wouldn't succeed.

Claire used a biblical picture of herself that had never occurred to me. She said that before her suicide attempt she had deeply identified with Samson in the Old Testament. Here is the picture to which she was referring: "Then the Philistines seized him, gouged out his eyes and took him down to Gaza. Binding him with bronze shackles, they set him to grinding in the prison" (Judges 16:21). Claire said she felt just like that—as if she were in a prison, strapped to a great grindstone, turning around and around, almost like a chained animal.

"I felt as if I was consigned to a treadmill. Whatever I tried took me in a vicious circle. Sometimes I could keep it under control and run slowly. But usually I'd get going faster and faster, because I felt driven to keep up. That is, to feel I was doing enough. But I never was, and so I never felt accepted or acceptable. I was trapped and couldn't find a way to get off. I got more and more worn out. I can understand why Samson ended up pulling the whole thing down. There didn't seem to be any way out...even today I wonder."

I've heard this kind of a desperate cry from many a sincere child of God who is "sick and tired of being sick and tired." That day I shared with Claire Luke 4:18-19— words conveying the strongest possible assurance of hope, words that fit so well her Samson picture, and spoken by Jesus as He began His ministry in the synagogue at Nazareth. The *New English Bible* renders these verses, "to proclaim release for prisoners...to let the broken victims go free." My prayer is that the good news of the Gospel of grace—the Lord's favor—may become a reality in your life.

R E F L E C T I O N

In what ways can you relate to Claire's despair and hopelessness? How do you feel about the hope offered in Luke 4:18-19?

Our Built-In
Warning System

"My guilt has overwhelmed me like a burden too heavy
to bear." *(Psalm 38:4)*

As any medical expert will tell you, pain is one of the best friends we have. It's the most valuable part of our built-in warning system.

Dr. Paul Brand worked for many years among the lepers of India, and he became highly skilled in rehabilitative surgery. He would attempt to repair the disease-eaten hands of lepers so that they could earn a living after they were cured. He discovered the main problem was the fact that the lepers felt no pain, and so were always seriously injuring their hands or feet.

After all kinds of experiments, he further discovered there was no way to restore sensitivity to pain once it was destroyed. Dr. Brand considers pain part of a brilliantly designed system and one of God's most amazing gifts to the human body. But he has also seen the cruelty of pain as he has watched patients die in unbearable agony.

Guilt is a form of mental and emotional pain we experience when we feel responsible for doing, or not doing, something which violates our personal moral standard. In that sense, it too is a gift of God to fallen and sinful human beings, and is intended to be part of His restraining and redeeming grace. Persons who have *no sense of guilt* are considered abnormal. They are called sociopaths or psychopaths, and many of them are dangerous. In a sense they are moral and spiritual lepers who have lost the ability to feel the pain of guilt.

But guilt can also go to the opposite extreme and become a cruel and destructive taskmaster. This is the kind of guilt so prevalent in the lives of performance-oriented Christians. For theirs are not the normal and specific feelings of guilt which come when they have done or thought something wrong. Instead, it is a vague and generalized emotion.

The constant pressure of their guilt keeps them trying to do and be more and more. Despite all the Scripture passages they know, and their many efforts to "trust and obey," they seem unable to shake off their feelings of guilt and to maintain an assurance that they are forgiven and acceptable to God.

REFLECTION

In what ways is guilt your taskmaster? At what times do you struggle most with feeling assurance of forgiveness and your acceptability to God?

Working Together

"Confess your sins to each other and pray for each other so that you may be healed."
(James 5:16a)

An amazing incident took place in Detroit in the summer of 1936. In order to accommodate the growing downtown traffic problems, city officials decided to widen Woodward Avenue. There was only one major problem: Central Methodist Church stood at the edge of Woodward Avenue. Since 1860 its great spire had pointed people toward God and it was a familiar city landmark.

The church fathers decided that they would cut off a portion of the church and then relocate the spire twenty-four feet to the east and six feet to the south! But with all its engineering genius, Detroit had no single machine strong enough and delicate enough to move that 2,000-ton spire.

Finally, a clever engineer came up with the solution. They would move the spire tower by putting seven great roller-jacks underneath it. Then they would select seven strong men who would learn to turn those jacks by hand in rhythmic unison. So they built the scaffolding and the huge jacks, and the men practiced together for days. The night before it was to be done, the engineer in charge slept in the park with his face turned all night toward that lonely tower—praying!

Before the city was awake they began the job. A

trained leader directed the men as they carefully turned all the jacks in precise unison; the spire moved four inches. Every morning for the next two weeks, the seven men turned their jacks until they had successfully moved that spire twenty-four feet east and six feet south! A group of people working together did what no one person—or machine—could do.

When Lazarus was restored to life, he was barely able to come out of the tomb. Jesus responded by saying: "Take off the grave clothes and let him go" (John 11:44). The message was plain: Jesus had done what only *He* could do. Now Lazarus' family and friends must do what only *they* could do.

The only way to remove the unhealthy, destructive, or sinful patterns from our past is through experiencing healthy, constructive personal relationships in the present.

R E F L E C T I O N

Identify some of your relationships where there is an atmosphere of intimacy and trust. What can you do to encourage openness in your closest relationships?

Waving a Red Flag

"Because He Himself suffered when He was tempted, He is able to help those who are being tempted."
(Hebrews 2:18)

Jesus must have realized that every person has his own set of predispositions when He warned His disciples, "Watch and pray so that you will not fall into temptation. The spirit is willing, but the body is weak" (Matthew 26:41).

Predispositions are those things within a person which are prior to his disposition, and which push it in a certain direction. These are the person's own private set of flags which, when waved before him, trigger off certain responses. These unchristianized complexes and unhealthy pushes from the past keep dragging us back and pulling us down. In spite of repenting and reading, pleading and praying, our childish responses keep playing the same old record.

One Sunday when we were serving Communion, the crowd was unusually large and it seemed to be taking far more time than normal. The longer it took, the more upset I got. I became overanxious and began to perspire. All of a sudden I saw myself as I really was and said, "This is utterly ridiculous. Here I am, standing here in my holy robe at the altar of the church, getting flustered because we are going to be a few minutes late."

And then I saw something else. I saw myself as a young boy with my schedule-maniac grandmother. She was the kind who had to be at the train station forty-five minutes ahead of schedule just to be on time. I could almost hear her prodding me, "Hurry up, David, what's taking you so long? Hurry up, or we'll be late." Then I prayed silently, "Lord, set me free from this. I do this every time something makes the service run over a few minutes, and I'm tired of letting that flustered little boy run my life."

I was able to relax and can say that it has not troubled me since. Up to then a tight schedule was like waving a red flag in my face—it produced in me a response of hurried overanxiety.

R E F L E C T I O N

What fears, resentments, and anxieties make up your private set of flags? What kinds of responses do your flags induce over and over again?

Please Don't
Leave Me!

"My God, my God, why have You forsaken me?"
(Psalm 22:1a)

etty's parents had been forced to get married because of her conception. It was an undesired marriage and Betty had been unwanted. When Betty was three and a half, her mother became pregnant again. However, her father had impregnated another woman at about the same time. This led to serious conflict and finally to divorce.

Betty vividly remembered that final day when her father walked out the door and left home. She remembered being in her own little crib-bed in the room when it happened; hearing the vicious quarrel and the terrifying moment when he left. It had left an aching, malignant core of pain deep within her. It was while we were in the midst of reexperiencing that incident during a time of prayer that the Lord took us right back into that crib.

During the healing time, Betty uttered a wracking, wrenching cry of pain which had been buried for many years. I said to her, "Betty, if you could have said something to your father from your crib, at that moment— what would you have said?" And suddenly the Holy Spirit brought into her memory exactly what she had felt in that moment of total desolation. And she cried out, not in the voice of a young adult, but the sobs of a three-and-a-half-year-old, "O Daddy, please don't leave me!" And all the terror and the pain of that moment came out "with sounds too deep to be uttered."

Later, it dawned on me that if we were to paraphrase Christ's cry from the cross ("My God, My God, why have You forsaken Me?") for a child, we couldn't improve on Betty's words: "Daddy, please don't leave me!"

And suddenly I realized that because of what Jesus experienced on that cross, He understands the cries heard so often today: "Daddy," or "Mommy," or "Honey, please don't leave me!" But they *do* leave. And the Wounded Healer understands those cries and is touched with the feelings of the child inside each of us.

R E F L E C T I O N

Has the Holy Spirit brought to light a deep hurt or pain that needs to be healed in your life? What has been the result of Him revealing that truth to you about your own brokenness?

Messed-Up People

"A father to the fatherless...is God in His holy dwelling."   *(Psalm 68:5)*

In the USA today, about 50% of those marrying for the first time will divorce. About 60% of those entering a second marriage will also divorce. In time about 75% of these divorced persons will get remarried. Because of this continuing disintegration of today's families, it is expected that by the year 2000 approximately one-half of the children of our country will spend part of their lives living with a stepparent and stepsiblings.

In the past few years of my counseling ministry, I have had to deal with some of the tragic complexities which arise from what modern sociologists call the "serial polygamy" of divorce and remarriage. As couples share with me their stories, I have no problem understanding about "his," "hers," and "our" children. But then I occasionally discover one who doesn't seem to fit any of those categories, who turns out to be a "divorce orphan," a child of a mate by a previous marriage who was left with one of the present partners when that prior husband or wife walked out and simply abandoned the child! Sometimes modern families are a complicated mess.

What is so amazing is that our God—the God of Abraham, Isaac, and Jacob—who chose such messed-up people to be His friends, seems to specialize in taking such menageries, mistakes, and messes and somehow making miracles out of them. God doesn't always do this the way we would want Him to—by instantly intervening in situations and changing the outer circumstances of people's lives so that they in turn can change. Most of the time, He implants in their lives a transformed outlook—a dream, a vision, a powerful conviction—which first changes them so that they are then enabled to live above the circumstances and become the means of changing situations.

R E F L E C T I O N

How would you describe the family situation from which you have come? Has God implanted a dream, vision, or conviction within you that allows you to live above difficult circumstances? In what way have you become the "means" of changing a difficult circumstance?

Shaking Grace Loose

"For it is commendable if a man bears up under the pain of unjust suffering because he is conscious of God."   (1 Peter 2:19)

Ted was an older seminary student who came to share some family problems with me. He had left a good job to obey God's call to the ministry, after he and his wife experienced dramatic conversions from what he called "the fast lane of Yuppie sin." Now he commuted every weekend to pastor two rural churches. He studied hard and visited his parishioners faithfully. He forcefully preached the transforming grace of God, saw lives changed, and watched the churches grow.

Then his eldest daughter began to rebel against this new life. She changed her lifestyle—clothes, hairdo, friends, language, habits—the works, and became an embarrassment to him in the seminary community and in his pastorate. Ted was amazed at how much he was beginning to resent his daughter. He was also feeling some anger at God—how could He let this happen, when they had sacrificed so much to answer the call to service?

As we talked, I began to suggest that although God did not *cause* the situation, He did want Ted to *learn* from it, to begin to understand the pain that the Heavenly Father must have felt when Ted was living in sin. And, most of all, to understand what love and grace are all about. Ted struggled with his feelings of anger and injustice, but slowly, he began to understand that God always accepts and loves us, even though He cannot approve of our behavior.

As Ted reached out to communicate grace to his daughter, he could see it was starting to make a difference in both of their lives. In our final time together, he was filled with deep emotion.

"You know," he said, "I've studied about God's grace, I've believed it with all my heart, I've preached about it regularly, and seen several people wonderfully changed by it. But I can see that it's been mostly in my head. Now God has allowed me to feel this kind of pain, because it's the only way He could shake grace loose from my head. It needed to be lowered about eighteen inches so I could experience it in my heart!"

R E F L E C T I O N

What are some times when you have struggled with feelings of anger and injustice toward God and others? Have you experienced grace at the heart level?

The Need to Understand

"Bear with each other and forgive whatever grievances you may have against one another. Forgive as the Lord forgave you."   *(Colossians 3:13)*

The worst case of child abuse I ever heard of was told to me by a man I counseled who had been verbally and physically abused by his mother. If you sat down and tried to conjure up ways of hurting and making a child miserable, you could not come up with more exquisite forms of cruelty.

Though he was now a grown man, he sobbed with bitter rage as he told me about it. When he was four, his mother made his favorite food, peanut butter and jelly sandwiches. Only she would throw them down, open-faced, on the kitchen floor, chop them into little pieces with a butcher knife and then tell him, "Get down and eat them off the floor—like the dog you are."

What bothered him most was the fact that he had been adopted. After sharing some particularly painful memory, he would often cry out, "But why, why did she want to adopt me if she was going to treat me like that? I can't figure it out."

One day I had to gently but firmly confront him with the fact that he might never be able to figure it out, and if he waited until he fully understood, he would probably never forgive her. It was a struggle, but during a long period of prayer he found the grace to forgive.

The need to psychoanalyze in order to understand

before we forgive is especially strong among children, particularly when the wrong involves their parents. It's terribly hard to face the fact that those who are supposed to love us can actually do things which hurt us so much. And so we feel we must analyze; we think that if we understand, we have forgiven. Don't make the mistake of confusing the two.

R E F L E C T I O N

In what ways have you confused the need to understand with forgiveness? Do you have a hard time forgiving wrongs that involve those close to you? Why or why not?

Nothing to Hide

"Therefore, since we have been justified through faith, we have peace with God through our Lord Jesus Christ."   *(Romans 5:1)*

A man named Stypulkowski was a fighter in the Polish underground resistance movement from 1939 to 1944. Unfortunately, when the war ended he was in the wrong place at the wrong time. He and fifteen other Poles were accused of helping the Nazis. They were taken to Russia to stand trial before a war crimes court for treason against the state. Actually, they had helped defeat the enemy with their tactics.

Prior to the trial, the men were put under rigorous interrogation to break them mentally, emotionally, and spiritually, to destroy their integrity so they would confess to anything demanded of them. Fifteen of the sixteen men broke under the grueling pressure. Only Stypulkowski stood firm. His tormentors relentlessly examined everything he had ever done, or hadn't done for its fear and guilt content—his work, his marriage, family, children, his sex life, his church and community life, even his concept of God.

This followed weeks of a starvation diet, sleepless nights, and calculated terror. Most insidious of all were the signed confessions of his best friends, all of whom blamed him. He was told his case was hopeless and was advised to plead guilty so his sentence would be lessened; otherwise, it was certain death.

But Stypulkowski refused. He said he had not been a traitor and could not confess to something which was not true. He went on to plead not guilty at his trial, and he was freed, largely because of the foreign observers there. Most impressive was the completely natural and unself-conscious way he witnessed to his Christian faith.

Because Stypulkowski could be totally honest about himself before God, he was able to be totally honest about himself before his accusers. He could freely admit his personal failures because he knew they had all been taken care of in the Cross.

And so with all of us. When we realize that being "justified through faith, we have peace with God," we will find the courage to face the truth about our needs, and experience healing grace.

R E F L E C T I O N
Do you have trouble being honest about yourself before God? Before others? Why or why not?

Confidence in
Our Leader

*"Those who are led by the Spirit of God are sons of
God."* (Romans 8:14)

M any people depend on feelings as the basis for
Christian guidance. One of the great promises
of the Christian life is found in Romans 8:14.
Nothing is more vital in life than the fact of God's guidance. But many of us misunderstand this to mean that
God always leads us by direct feelings and inner impressions.

Some Christians go to ridiculous lengths on these
things. This perpetual praying for a feeling or an inner
voice on what to do runs all the way from the smallest
daily decisions to the most serious matters of life. Now
the error occurs not about the fact that God does indeed
speak through the subjective inner voice, through feelings and impressions. I have had experiences when God
did speak that way. The error lies in making feelings and
impressions the main source of God's guidance,
unchecked and unbalanced with the other, more regular
ways in which God guides us.

Feelings and impressions come from three sources:
from God, from the devil, and from the inner workings of
our minds—our personality patterns, temperament and
disposition, emotional hangups and scars, from the damaged emotions of our lives. This third source can be used
by either the Holy Spirit or Satan.

If you are a child of God, the Holy Spirit lives in you,

and as long as you are walking in the right path, obeying the directions of the Lord, you may not hear any special voice of guidance, because you do not need it. To stop and expect some feeling or impression on every simple detail of daily life is a vote of no confidence in the Holy Spirit who indwells you.

R E F L E C T I O N

What emotional factors in your life might allow you to be misguided by feelings and inner impressions? Are you living on the assumption that what you are doing is right because you are led by the Spirit? Why or why not?

Assuming
Responsibility

---

*"Do not conform any longer to the pattern of this world,
but be transformed by the renewing of your mind."*
                                              (Romans 12:2a)

There is an inseparable connection between forgiving others and assuming responsibility for
our lives. God taught me this the hard way.
In my early Christian life, for many more years than I
like to admit, I felt as if I never made a mistake or failed
at anything I did. Not literally, of course. Yes, I blew it, I
failed, I made terrible mistakes and I fell. But not really,
because it wasn't really me. For every time I failed or fell
or missed the mark, there was a little photoelectric cell
that automatically turned on the current inside of my
brain. I could almost hear it go *ping* when it switched on.
And a light came on, and then a tiny voice inside me
whispered, *That's OK, David. Sure, you blew it, you
made a mistake, but don't worry about it. You wouldn't
have done that if you had had a different mother.*

I didn't have to flip a switch—it came on by itself. I'm
ashamed to say I lived with that and believed it for many
years. It was a down-filled comforter that cushioned me
whenever I fell. But when God led me into my own personal experience of deep inner healing, I had to wade
through the waters of forgiveness. And that was one of
the first things He pointed out to me.

"David, that's got to go. From now on it's just you and
Me, with no one to blame. You must assume full responsi-

bility for your life—your choices, your attitudes, and actions. From now on they're all yours."

In the beginning I found that terribly difficult, for the old light and voice would automatically switch on. I had to deliberately turn them off and break a habit of many years. I had to intentionally work at *owning my choices* and *assuming full responsibility* for my life. This was a vital part of the forgiving process.

R E F L E C T I O N

What automatic switches go on when you fail or make mistakes? Have you owned your choices and assumed full responsibility for your life? Why or why not?

Sticking with Your Dream

"May He give you the desire of your heart and make all your plans succeed."   *(Psalm 20:4)*

For as long as he could remember, Arnett had dreamed of being a civil engineer. One day he heard that an engineering college in Ohio had a co-op course in civil engineering where he could work his way through. He thrived on this outdoor railroad work and was as tough and godless as the next guy in the crew. But he had a Christian uncle who took a deep interest in him.

One summer vacation, Uncle John invited Arnett to attend Camp Sychar, near Mount Vernon, Ohio. Thinking it was a summer youth camp where he might meet some pretty girls, Arnett gladly accepted. Imagine his shock when it turned out to be an old-fashioned camp meeting with three preaching services a day.

On Missionary Day, a well-known bishop from China described the people's need for Christ as well as China's great need for roads, bridges, and buildings—the very thing Arnett was specializing in. Arnett began daydreaming of going to China as an engineer.

Suddenly his daydream was rudely interrupted. A strange sensation—something, someone—seemed to be talking to him. But then, stretching across the top of the platform above the speaker's head, there appeared a vision. One word was spelled out in fiery, silver letters: INDIA. An inner voice was saying, "No, not China. I want you to be a missionary in India."

It was all over in a matter of seconds, but it left Arnett physically and emotionally shaken with fear, but mostly anger.

"How dare You (yes, of course, it was God—he knew that instinctively) interfere with my plans? A missionary to India? I'm not even a Christian!"

That's quite a story, isn't it? But it really happened. For you see, that young man was my dad, who was converted *after* his call to service. Who, in spite of the strong advice most Christians gave him, did not quit engineering school and go to seminary. Instead, he stuck to his dream and finished his civil engineering degree. He said he "could not be disobedient to that heavenly vision." And he did become an "Engineer-Evangelist" missionary to India and served there for more than forty years. He led thousands to Christ and built over 100 churches as well as hospitals and schools.

R E F L E C T I O N

What is the most important dream or desire of your life? What would it take to stick to your dream?

Contemplating the Cross

"In Him was life, and that life was the light of men."
(John 1:4)

During my thirty years of counseling at Asbury, I kept the same painting hanging on the wall so that my counselees would face it. It was a large copy of Salvador Dali's *Christ of St. John of the Cross.* It is an unusual portrayal of the Crucifixion. Instead of looking up at the cross from ground level, the painting looks down from above, as if from God's perspective. The cross is massive and seems to loom over the whole world. Jesus is pictured as young and strong and holding back the darkness that surrounds Him. In the foreground, the earth, the sky, and the sea are all lit with the light streaming forth from the cross. It's as if we are seeing the whole world through its light.

During those years there were hundreds of occasions when counselees seemed to reach an impasse. Sometimes it was because of the terrifying memories of abuse, betrayal, abandonment, or rejection, the sins against them which kept them from moving on. Other times it was the heavy burden of guilt and shame from their own sins. Often it was a complex intertwining of both.

Whenever we reached that place, I always turned toward the painting and asked the person to join me in focusing attention on it. Sometimes there would be several minutes of silence as we did what the mystics of earlier centuries advised, "Contemplate the cross." I knew that if only the meaning and message of that scene would get through to them, things could change, because everything looks different in the light of the cross. For in its light, we see most clearly the One whom John described as "full of grace and truth" (John 1:14). And in its light we also see clearly the truth about ourselves and about God's grace for us.

In its light, the line from "Amazing Grace" becomes true for us: " 'Twas grace that taught my heart to fear, and grace my fears relieved!" Times without number, that sight and that light broke the deadlock, and became the turning point in the process of healing.

R E F L E C T I O N

Have you taken time to "contemplate the cross"? What truths have you learned about yourself? About God's grace? If you chose to look at everything in the light of the cross, how would your life be changed?

Scripture Index

Source Index